# EVOLVE

## WORKBOOK

Samuela Eckstut

CAMBRIDGE
UNIVERSITY PRESS

Shaftesbury Road, Cambridge CB2 8EA, United Kingdom

One Liberty Plaza, 20th Floor, New York, NY 10006, USA

477 Williamstown Road, Port Melbourne, VIC 3207, Australia

314–321, 3rd Floor, Plot 3, Splendor Forum, Jasola District Centre, New Delhi – 110025, India

103 Penang Road, #05–06/07, Visioncrest Commercial, Singapore 238467

Cambridge University Press & Assessment is a department of the University of Cambridge.

We share the University's mission to contribute to society through the pursuit of education, learning and research at the highest international levels of excellence.

www.cambridge.org
Information on this title: www.cambridge.org/9781108408943

© Cambridge University Press & Assessment 2019

First published 2019

20  19  18  17  16

Printed in Malaysia by Vivar Printing

*A catalogue record for this publication is available from the British Library*

ISBN 978-1-108-40521-8 Student's Book
ISBN 978-1-108-40503-4 Student's Book A
ISBN 978-1-108-40914-8 Student's Book B
ISBN 978-1-108-40522-5 Student's Book with Practice Extra
ISBN 978-1-108-40504-1 Student's Book with Practice Extra A
ISBN 978-1-108-40915-5 Student's Book with Practice Extra B
ISBN 978-1-108-40894-3 Workbook with Audio
ISBN 978-1-108-40859-2 Workbook with Audio A
ISBN 978-1-108-41191-2 Workbook with Audio B
ISBN 978-1-108-40512-6 Teacher's Edition with Test Generator
ISBN 978-1-108-41062-5 Presentation Plus
ISBN 978-1-108-41201-8 Class Audio CDs
ISBN 978-1-108-40791-5 Video Resource Book with DVD
ISBN 978-1-108-41200-1 Full Contact with DVD
ISBN 978-1-108-41152-3 Full Contact with DVD A
ISBN 978-1-108-41410-4 Full Contact with DVD B

Additional resources for this publication at www.cambridge.org/evolvet

# CONTENTS

# UNIT **1**    I AM ...

## 1.1    I'M BRAZILIAN. AND YOU?

### 1  VOCABULARY: Countries and nationalities

A  **Read and complete the sentences.**

1  I'm _____Peruvian_____ . I'm from Lima in Peru.

2  I'm Japanese. I'm from Tokyo in _____Japan_____ .

3  I'm from Tegucigalpa in _____ . I'm Honduran.

4  I'm _____ . I'm from Madrid in Spain.

5  I'm from Medellín in _____ . I'm Colombian.

6  I'm _____ . I'm from Rio de Janeiro in Brazil.

7  I'm from Beijing in _____ . I'm Chinese.

8  I'm _____ . I'm from Moscow in Russia.

9  I'm from Miami in _____ . I'm American.

10  I'm from Seoul in South Korea. I'm _____ .

11  I'm _____ . I'm from Santiago in Chile.

12  I'm _____ . I'm from Mexico City in Mexico.

13  I'm from Quito in Ecuador. I'm _____ .

14  I'm _____ . I'm from Paris in France.

### 2  GRAMMAR: *I am, you are*

A  Circle the correct words.

1  I *am* / *are* Mexican.

2  *Am* / *Are* you from Russia?

3  *Am* / *Are* you María?

4  No, I *'m* / *'re* Diana.

5  You *'m* / *'re* not Ivan.

6  Yes, I *'m* / *'re* in Seoul!

B **Complete the conversation. Use the words in the box.**

| 'm | are | ~~are you~~ | I am |
|----|-----|---------|------|
| I'm | I'm not | you | you're |

**Tony** [1] _____Are you_____ Ana?

**Ana** Yes, [2] _____.

**Tony** Hi, [3] _____ Tony. I'm from Lima.

**Ana** Oh, [4] _____ Peruvian. I [5] _____ Brazilian.

**Tony** [6] _____ you from Rio?

**Ana** No, [7] _____. I'm not from Rio or São Paulo.

**Tony** Are [8] _____ from Brasília?

**Ana** Yes.

## 3 GRAMMAR AND VOCABULARY

A **Write true sentences for you.**

1 teacher  _I'm not a teacher._

2 student  _I'm a student._

3 Mexico City _____

4 American _____

5 Alex _____

6 Chile _____

FIND IT

B **Think of three famous people. Write affirmative (+) and negative (−) sentences.**

Lionel Messi

> Hi. I'm Lionel Messi. I'm not from Spain. I'm Argentinian.

> Hi. I'm Michelle Obama. I'm American. I'm not from Washington, D.C. I'm from Chicago.

Michelle Obama

3

## 1   VOCABULARY: The alphabet; personal information

A   🔊 **1.01** **Listen and write the words the speakers spell.**

1   👂     Palmira

2   👂

3   👂

4   👂

5   👂

B   **Match 1–5 with a–e.**

| | | | | |
|---|---|---|---|---|
| 1 | Harvard University | *d* | a | email address |
| 2 | Toyota | | b | first name |
| 3 | tonyravella@mymail.org | | c | company |
| 4 | Ravella | | d | college |
| 5 | Tony | | e | last name |

C   **Make sentences with the words from exercise 1B.**

1    My *college* is Harvard University.

2

3

4

5

## 2 GRAMMAR: *What's . . . ? It's . . .*

A **Read 1–6. Check (✓) *Question* or *Answer*.**

|   |                                    | Question | Answer |
|---|------------------------------------|----------|--------|
| 1 | What's your first name?            | ✔        |        |
| 2 | It's Nippon College.               |          |        |
| 3 | What's the name of your company?   |          |        |
| 4 | What's your last name?             |          |        |
| 5 | It's Higuera.                      |          |        |
| 6 | It's cccomputers@mymail.org.       |          |        |

B **Complete the questions and answers.**

1 _____ your first name? _____ Mike.

2 _____ your last name? _____ Ramirez.

3 _____ the name of your _____? It's Nippon College.

## 3 GRAMMAR AND VOCABULARY

A **Find and correct <u>three</u> mistakes in the conversation.**

**Anna** Hello. What your last name?

**Mike** It's Lugo. L-U-G-O.

**Anna** Uh-huh. What's your first name?

**Mike** It Mike.

**Anna** And what's your email address?

**Mike** Its mikelugo@mymail.org.

B **Answer the questions for you.**

1 What's your last name? _____

2 What's your first name? _____

3 What's your email address? _____

# 1.3 THIS IS THE KEY

## 1 FUNCTIONAL LANGUAGE: Checking into a hotel

A **Complete the conversation. Use the words in the box.**

| cell phone number | It's | last | nights | room |
|---|---|---|---|---|
| sign | This is | ~~Welcome~~ | what's | |

**Clerk** Hello. ¹ _____Welcome_____ to the Capital Hotel.

**Anna** Hello. I'm Anna. I'm here for two ² _____ .

**Clerk** What's your ³ _____ name, Anna?

**Anna** It's Wang. W-A-N-G.

**Clerk** Ah, yes. Anna Wang. What's your ⁴ _____ , Anna?

**Anna** It's (243) 555–1968.

**Clerk** And ⁵ _____ your email address?

**Anna** ⁶ _____ wang99@mymail.org.

**Clerk** Thank you. One moment. Please ⁷ _____ here.

**Anna** OK.

**Clerk** ⁸ _____ the key. You're in ⁹ _____ 10F.

**Anna** Great. Thank you.

**Clerk** You're welcome.

## 2 REAL-WORLD STRATEGY: Checking spelling

A **Dan is at a hotel. The clerk asks about spelling. Write the questions.**

1 **Dan** I'm Dan Gonzales.

  **Clerk** _____

  **Dan** G-O-N-Z-A-L-E-S.

2 **Dan** My email address is dgonza14@mail.org.

  **Clerk** _____

  **Dan** D-G-O-N-Z-A-14 at M-A-I-L dot O-R-G.

3 **Dan** I'm from Martin Hotel Company.

  **Clerk** _____

  **Dan** M-A-R-T-I-N.

## 3 FUNCTIONAL LANGUAGE AND REAL-WORLD STRATEGY

A   Read the sentences. Who says each sentence? Check (✓) the correct column.

| | A hotel clerk | A hotel guest | A hotel clerk OR a hotel guest |
|---|---|---|---|
| 1   Hello. | | | ✔ |
| 2   Welcome to City Hotel. | | | |
| 3   What's your name? | | | |
| 4   How do you spell your last name? | | | |
| 5   I'm here for one night. | | | |
| 6   What's your cell phone number? | | | |
| 7   Here's the key. | | | |
| 8   You're in room 316. | | | |
| 9   Thank you. | | | |
| 10   You're welcome. | | | |
| 11   My name is Robert Dupont. | | | |

B   Write a conversation between a hotel clerk and a hotel guest. Use the sentences in exercise 3A and the conversations on page 6 to help you. Add <u>one</u> question from the hotel clerk.

## 1   VOCABULARY: Jobs

A   Look at the pictures and read the conversations. Circle an answer (*a* or *b*). Write the correct job in *b*.

**1**   Are you a salesperson?
   **a**   Yes, I am.
   **b**   No, I'm not. I'm a
     _____ .

**2**   Are you an artist?
   **a**   Yes, I am.
   **b**   No, I'm not. I'm a
     _____ .

**3**   Are you a teacher?
   **a**   Yes, I am.
   **b**   No, I'm not. I'm a
     _____ .

**4**   Are you a hotel clerk?
   **a**   Yes, I am.
   **b**   No, I'm not. I'm a
     _____ .

## 2   READING

A   **READ FOR DETAILS**   Read the profile. Check (✓) the information in the profile.

My name is David Pérez Delgado. David is my first name. Pérez and Delgado are my last names. In the United States my last name is Pérez. I'm a salesperson in Mexico. I'm from Mexico City. I'm an English student at a school in Texas. The name of the school is Texas International Language School. My teacher is from Austin, Texas. She is American.

**1**   nationality      _____
**2**   last name      _____
**3**   email address      _____

**4**   job in Mexico      _____
**5**   the name of the English school      _____
**6**   the name of the English teacher      _____

## 3 WRITING

**A** Complete the conversations. Use *Hello, Hi,* or *Hey.*

1  Teacher _____ My name is Mr. Hewson. You're new here.

   Student _____ Yes. I'm a new student. My name is Yasuhiro Momoto.

2  Student _____ Yasu. How are you? Are you a student here?

   Student _____ Jaime. Yes, I am. How are you?

**B** Change the sentences. Use capital letters and periods.

1  i'm emma durand  _____ I'm Emma Durand.

2  i'm a french chef

3  my home is in new york

4  i'm from paris in france

5  i'm french and american

6  i'm a teacher

7  the name of the school is new york chef school

8  my students are from the united states, canada, mexico, and japan

**C** How are you and Emma Durand different? Write <u>four</u> sentences.

I'm not Emma Durand. I'm Lisa Santiago.

# CHECK AND REVIEW

**Read the statements. Can you do these things?**

| UNIT 1 | Mark the boxes. ☑ I can do it.  ? I am not sure.<br>I can ... | If you are not sure, go back to these pages in the Student's Book. |
|---|---|---|
| VOCABULARY | ☐ use words for countries and nationalities. | page 2 |
| | ☐ use the alphabet. | page 5 |
| | ☐ use words for personal information. | page 5 |
| | ☐ use words for numbers. | page 6 |
| | ☐ use words for jobs. | page 8 |
| GRAMMAR | ☐ use *I am* and *you are.* | page 3 |
| | ☐ ask and answer questions with *What's ... ?* and *It's ...* | page 5 |
| FUNCTIONAL LANGUAGE | ☐ check into a hotel. | page 6 |
| | ☐ check spelling. | page 7 |
| SKILLS | ☐ write a personal profile. | page 9 |
| | ☐ use capital letters and periods. | page 9 |

# UNIT 2  GREAT PEOPLE

## 2.1  A FAMILY PARTY

**1  VOCABULARY: Family; numbers**

A  **You are Bill. Look at the family tree. Then write the family words in 2–12.**

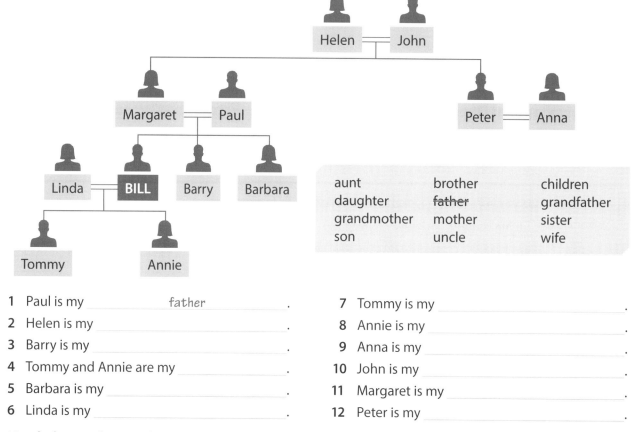

| aunt | brother | children |
| daughter | ~~father~~ | grandfather |
| grandmother | mother | sister |
| son | uncle | wife |

1  Paul is my _____father_____ .

2  Helen is my _____ .

3  Barry is my _____ .

4  Tommy and Annie are my _____ .

5  Barbara is my _____ .

6  Linda is my _____ .

7  Tommy is my _____ .

8  Annie is my _____ .

9  Anna is my _____ .

10  John is my _____ .

11  Margaret is my _____ .

12  Peter is my _____ .

B  **Match the numbers and words.**

| 13 | sixty-five | 18 | eleven | 47 | seventy-one | 16 | eighteen | fifteen |

| one hundred | twenty-four | 82 | fourteen | 19 | 60 | twenty-nine |

| fifty-five | 94 | 88 | 30 | ten | 55 | 29 | 70 | 50 | sixty |

| forty-six | 65 | eighty-two | forty-seven | ninety-three | 46 | thirty-nine |

| ninety-four | thirteen | thirty | 100 | 15 | 93 | eighty-eight | 11 | twelve |

| seventy | sixteen | fifty | nineteen | 12 | 24 | 71 | 10 | 39 | 14 |

## 2 GRAMMAR: *is / are* in statements and *yes/no* questions

A Complete the sentences with *is* or *are*.

Hello. My name ¹ _____ is _____ Tamara. My family and I
² _____ Colombian. We ³ _____ from
Bogotá. My grandparents ⁴ _____ from Medellín.
My father ⁵ _____ a teacher, and my mother
⁶ _____ an artist. My brothers ⁷ _____
19 and 14. My sister ⁸ _____ 21. My sister and I
⁹ _____ college students.

B Write questions and answers about Tamara. Use the words in parentheses ( ).

1 (your name / Rosaria)
   Is your name Rosaria?
   No, it isn't. It's Tamara.

2 (you and your family / Colombian)

3 (you / from Medellín)

4 (your grandparents / from Medellín)

5 (your father / an artist)

6 (your sister / 21)

C Write two more questions about Tamara.
   1 _____
   2 _____

## 3 GRAMMAR AND VOCABULARY

A Read the answers. Write questions about <u>your</u> family.

1 Is your mother American?        No, she's not.
2 Are your cousins here?          No, they're not.
3 _____                           Yes, he is.
4 _____                           Yes, she is.
5 _____                           Yes, we are.
6 _____                           Yes, they are.
7 _____                           No, we're not.
8 _____                           No, he's not.

### 1 VOCABULARY: Describing people; *really / very*

**A** Write the correct adjectives from the box for the pictures.

| boring | friendly | funny | interesting | ~~old~~ |
| short | shy | smart | tall | young |

1 ___old___   3 _____   5 _____
2 _____   4 _____   6 _____

7 _____   8 _____   9 _____   10 _____

**B** Circle the correct answer.

1
   a Her husband is tall.
   b Her husband is really tall.
   c Her husband isn't very tall.

2
   a Nicolas is boring.
   b Nicolas is really boring.
   c Nicolas isn't very boring.

3
   a My brother isn't very shy.
   b My brother isn't shy.
   c My brother is very shy.

4
   a Celia is smart.
   b Celia isn't smart.
   c Celia isn't very smart.

**2** GRAMMAR: *is not / are not*

A   **Complete the sentences. Use *'s, is, 're, are,* or *isn't, aren't* or *not*.**

1   Sachi is from Los Angeles. _____She's not_____ from Peru.

2   My uncle's not very interesting. _____ boring.

3   My brother and I are in college. _____ very smart.

4   He _____ really tall, but I'm short.

5   My children are 2 and 4. _____ very old.

6   Joe is my dog. _____ really friendly!

B   **Write the sentences again. Use *'s not, isn't, 're not,* and *aren't*.**

1   You are not boring. You are funny.
    *You're not boring. You're funny!*

2   My sister is not tall, and she is not old. She is five.
    _____

3   My husband and I are not from Mexico, and we are not from Canada. We are from the United States.
    _____

4   Mr. May is not my teacher, and he is not your teacher. He is the chef at our school.
    _____

5   Dr. Norton is not here, and she is not at home. She is at the college.
    _____

6   Rita and Lara are not sisters, and they are not cousins. They are friends.
    _____

**3** GRAMMAR AND VOCABULARY

A   **Write true sentences. Use the words in the box.**

| My parents | | | boring |
|---|---|---|---|
| My mother | | | friendly |
| My father | | | funny |
| My grandparents | is | | interesting |
| My cousins | isn't | really | old |
| My sister | are | very | short |
| My brother | aren't | | shy |
| My best friend | | | smart |
| My teacher | | | tall |
| | | | young |

1   *My mother isn't very tall. My father is tall.*   6   _____
2   _____   7   _____
3   _____   8   _____
4   _____   9   _____
5   _____

# WHEN IS YOUR BIRTHDAY?

**1** FUNCTIONAL LANGUAGE: Asking about and saying ages and birthdays

A **Read the sentences (a–h). Then write a conversation for Diego, Anna, and Sophia.**

   a   Happy birthday, Diego!

   b   Oh, right! You're seven this month? Happy birthday from me!

   c   Oh, wow! When is your birthday, Sophia?

   d   Thanks. Oh, Anna. This is my daughter, Sophia.

   e   I'm six, and my brother is three years old.

   f   ~~Today is my birthday.~~

   g   Hello, Sophia. My name is Anna. How old are you?

   h   It's on December 5.

| Diego | Today is my birthday. | Sophia | _____ |
|-------|----------------------|--------|------------|
| Anna  | _____           | Anna   | _____ |
| Diego | _____           | Sophia | _____ |
| Anna  | _____           | Anna   | _____ |

B **Look at the <u>underlined</u> numbers. Write the words.**

| 1 | He's <u>4</u>.  | four | His birthday is February <u>4</u>. | fourth |
|---|-----------------|------|-----------------------------------|--------|
| 2 | She's <u>30</u>. |      | Her birthday is April <u>30</u>.   |        |
| 3 | He's <u>1</u>.  |      | His birthday is January <u>1</u>.  |        |
| 4 | She's <u>22</u>. |      | Her birthday is March <u>22</u>.   |        |
| 5 | I'm <u>31</u>.  |      | My birthday is July <u>31</u>.     |        |
| 6 | She's <u>3</u>. |      | Her birthday is June <u>3</u>.     |        |
| 7 | He's <u>27</u>. |      | His birthday is May <u>27</u>.     |        |
| 8 | She's <u>18</u>. |      | Her birthday is August <u>18</u>.  |        |

## 2 REAL-WORLD STRATEGY: Correcting yourself

A **Read the sentences. Correct the mistakes with information in the box. Use *No, sorry,* or *Sorry, I mean*.**

> Alexa—12, March 2       Cecilia—15, May 30
> Sandra—19, April 30     Ariana—21, September 13

1 It's my sister Alexa's birthday today. She's 13.
_____ No, sorry, 12. _____

2 My sister Cecilia is 15. Her birthday is April 30.
_____

3 My sister Sandra's birthday is April 30. She's 17.
_____

4 Ariana is 21. Her birthday is November 13.
_____

## 3 FUNCTIONAL LANGUAGE AND REAL-WORLD STRATEGY

A **Use the words in the box to complete the conversation.**

> mean   old   sorry   when   years

**Paul**        This is my niece, Olivia.

**Gabriela**    Hi, Olivia! How ¹_____ are you?

**Olivia**      I'm 10. Sorry, I ²_____ nine. I'm nine years and eleven months old.

**Gabriela**    You're a tall girl! ³_____ is your birthday?

**Olivia**      It's June 31.

**Gabriela**    June 31?

**Olivia**      No, ⁴_____, July 31.

**Gabriela**    Oh. So you're 9 ⁵_____ old, and your birthday is July 31.

B **Write a conversation between you and Gabriela about the ages of people in your family.**

**Gabriela**    _____ My brother is 18 years old. _____      **Gabriela**    _____

**You**         _____                          **You**         _____

**Gabriela**    _____                          **Gabriela**    _____

**You**         _____                          **You**         _____

# HERE'S MY BAND

## 1 LISTENING

A  ◀) **2.01**  **LISTEN FOR GIST**  What do the people do together?

1 _____

2 _____

3 _____

4 _____

5 _____ Flora _____

B  ◀) **2.01**  **LISTEN FOR DETAIL**  Write the names of the people in the photo: *Aniko, Tony, Claudia,* and *Zack*.

C  ◀) **2.01**  **LISTEN FOR DETAIL**  Complete the sentences with names from the photo.

1 _____ Zack _____ is 23.

2 _____ is from Los Angeles.

3 _____ is an artist.

4 _____ is really friendly.

5 _____ is a doctor.

6 _____ is 28.

## 2 GRAMMAR: Prepositions of place

A  **Read the sentences about the picture in exercise 1. Circle the correct words.**

1 Aniko is *between / on the right* Claudia and Zack.

2 Tony is *in / on* the left.

3 Claudia is *next / next to* Tony.

4 We're *at / in* Chicago.

5 Flora isn't next to *I / me.*

## 3 WRITING

**A** **Read the sentences. <u>Underline</u> *and* when it joins words. (Circle) *and* when it joins sentences.**

1 We are from different countries, (and) we are different ages.

2 Jiyoung <u>and</u> I are from South Korea.

3 Three students are 19, (and) eight students are 20.

4 Klaus is from Germany, (and) he is a chef.

5 Klaus is between Jiyoung <u>and</u> me.

6 The teacher is interesting <u>and</u> funny.

**B** **Read about the people. Join <u>four</u> sentences. Use *and*.**

My friends and I are from different countries. We are different ages. I am from France. Jiyoung and Jinho are from South Korea. One friend is from China. Two friends are from Brazil. Yi is from China. Yi and I are artists. I'm 22. Yi is 24.

1  My friends and I are from different countries, and we are different ages.

2  _____

3  _____

4  _____

5  _____

**C** **Write about three people in your class. How old are they? Who is: next to you, on the left, on the right, and between you and another student? Use *and* to join words and sentences.**

# CHECK AND REVIEW

**Read the statements. Can you do these things?**

| UNIT 2 | Mark the boxes.   ☑ I can do it.   ? I am not sure.<br>I can … | If you are not sure, go back to these pages in the Student's Book. |
|---|---|---|
| VOCABULARY | ☐ use words for family members. | page 12 |
| | ☐ say numbers. | page 12 |
| | ☐ use adjectives to describe people. | page 14 |
| | ☐ use *really* and *very*. | page 14 |
| GRAMMAR | ☐ use *is* and *are* in statements and *yes/no* questions. | page 13 |
| | ☐ use *is not* and *are not*. | page 15 |
| | ☐ use prepositions of place. | page 18 |
| FUNCTIONAL LANGUAGE | ☐ ask about and say people's ages and birthdays. | page 16 |
| | ☐ correct myself. | page 17 |
| SKILLS | ☐ write a description of the people in my class. | page 19 |
| | ☐ use *and* to connect words and sentences. | page 19 |

### 1   VOCABULARY: Rooms in a home

**A**   **Look at the apartment plan and read the words. Then correct the mistakes in sentences 2–10 below.**

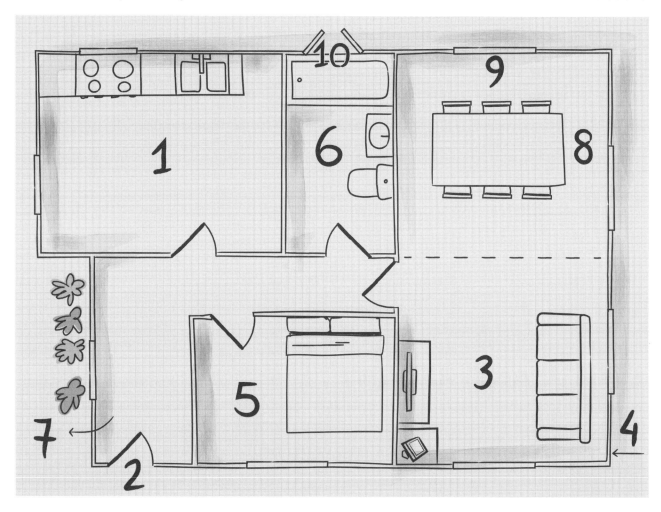

1   This is the living room.   <u>No, it's the kitchen.</u>
2   This is the floor.
3   This is the dining area.
4   This is a picture.
5   This is a bathroom.
6   This is a bedroom.
7   This is the door.
8   This is the kitchen.
9   This is a window.
10   This is a wall.

## 2 GRAMMAR: Possessive adjectives; possessive 's and s'

A **Circle the correct words.**

1 I'm Mr. Costa. *My* / *His* / *Your* first name is Ricardo.
2 We are from Mexico. *Your* / *Their* / *Our* home is in Oaxaca.
3 My cousins are artists. These are *my* / *their* / *his* pictures.
4 Johann has three children. That's *his* / *your* / *her* daughter.
5 Are you married? Where is *your* / *my* / *his* wife?
6 Ms. Montero is an art teacher. *Her* / *My* / *Your* class is in Room 116.

B **Complete the sentences with possessive words.**

1 My parents sleep in this room.      It's ___my parents'___ bedroom.
2 Jonathan lives in this house.       It's _____ house.
3 Her aunt has a picture on the wall.  It's her _____ picture.
4 The students have eight books.      They are the _____ books.
5 Her cousins have a friendly dog.    That's her _____ dog.
6 Sari has a new email address.       What's _____ email address?

## 3 GRAMMAR AND VOCABULARY

A **Write sentences about your home or your friends' homes. Use the words in parentheses ( ).**

1 (bedroom / big)          ___My bedroom is big. OR My bedroom isn't big.___
2 (dining area / next to)  _____
3 (kitchen / new)          _____
4 (picture / interesting)  _____
5 (living room / small)    _____
6 (bathroom / between)     _____

# 3.2 | IS IT REALLY A CHAIR?

## 1 VOCABULARY: Furniture

A **Look at the letters in A. Write the furniture in B. Write the name of the room in C.**

| A Letters | B Furniture | C Room / Rooms |
|---|---|---|
| 1 sked | *desk* | *living room or bedroom* |
| 2 koobseac | | |
| 3 niks | | |
| 4 gur | | |
| 5 hersow | | |
| 6 VT | | |
| 7 malp | | |
| 8 ebd | | |
| 9 irach | | |
| 10 bleat | | |
| 11 gerretirfoar | | |
| 12 ochuc | | |

## 2 GRAMMAR: *It is*

A **Look at the pictures. Complete the sentences. Use 's, is, isn't, it's, or it's not.**

1 The bookcase _____isn't_____ in the living room. _____It's_____ in the dining area.
2 The lamp _____ in the bedroom. _____ in the living room.
3 The TV _____ in the bedroom. _____ in the kitchen.
4 The couch _____ in the living room. _____ in the bedroom.
5 _____ the table in the kitchen? No, _____ in the dining area.
6 _____ the bed in the bedroom? Yes, _____ in the bedroom.

B Complete the conversation. Use *is*, *isn't*, *it's*, *it is*, *it's not*, or *is it …*?

**Lucy** This is our home. [1] ___It's___ in Toronto.

**Hyun** [2] _____ an apartment?

**Lucy** No, [3] _____ . [4] _____ a house.

**Hyun** [5] _____ big?

**Lucy** No. [6] _____ small.

**Hyun** [7] _____ new?

**Lucy** Yes, [8] _____ . And it's very nice. Is your home in Seoul?

**Hyun** My home [9] _____ in Seoul. It's in Busan. And [10] _____ an apartment, not a house. The apartment [11] _____ very big, but our small apartment is OK.

## 3 GRAMMAR AND VOCABULARY

A Read the words in the boxes. Then make sentences about your home.

**Furniture**

| bed | bookcase | chair | couch | desk | lamp |
| refrigerator | rug | shower | sink | table | TV |

**Rooms**

bathroom    bedroom    dining area    kitchen    living room

**Adjectives**

| big | cool | good | great | new |
| nice | old | short | small | tall |

1 The desk in my bedroom isn't very old.
2 _____
3 _____
4 _____
5 _____
6 _____
7 _____
8 _____
9 _____
10 _____

# 3.3 COFFEE OR TEA?

**1** FUNCTIONAL LANGUAGE: Making and replying to offers; accepting a drink and snack

A **Look at what Dan, Coco, and Dalia want. Then write the conversations below. Use the words in the box.**

**Dan**     tea, sugar (1), cookie
**Coco**    coffee
**Dalia**    tea, sugar (2), milk, cookie

| cookie | coffee | tea | milk | sugar |
|--------|--------|-----|------|-------|

**1**

| | |
|---|---|
| **You** | *Coffee or tea?* |
| **Dan** | *Tea, please.* |
| **You** | *With milk?* |
| **Dan** | *No, thanks.* |
| **You** | *With sugar?* |
| **Dan** | *Sure. One, please.* |
| **You** | *A cookie?* |
| **Dan** | *Yes, please.* |
| **You** | *Here you are.* |
| **Dan** | *Thank you.* |

**2**

| | |
|---|---|
| **You** | *Coffee or tea?* |
| **Coco** | *Coffee, please.* |
| **You** | *With milk?* |
| **Coco** | |
| **You** | *Sugar?* |
| **Coco** | |
| **You** | *A cookie?* |
| **Coco** | |
| **You** | *Here you are.* |
| **Coco** | |

**3**

| | |
|---|---|
| **You** | *Coffee or tea?* |
| **Dalia** | |
| **You** | |
| **Dalia** | |
| **You** | |
| **Dalia** | |
| **You** | |
| **Dalia** | |
| **You** | |
| **Dalia** | |

## 2 REAL-WORLD STRATEGY: Asking about words you don't understand

A 🔊 **3.01** **Listen to the conversation. Then check (✓) *True* or *False*.**

|   |   | True | False |
|---|---|------|-------|
| 1 | Jason wants coffee. | ☐ | ☐ |
| 2 | Jason wants milk. | ☐ | ☐ |
| 3 | Jason wants sugar. | ☐ | ☐ |
| 4 | Jason understands *biscuit*. | ☐ | ☐ |
| 5 | Jason wants a cookie. | ☐ | ☐ |

## 3 FUNCTIONAL LANGUAGE AND REAL-WORLD STRATEGY

A **Correct the <u>four</u> mistakes in the conversation.**

**Lina**   Coffee or tea?

**Jason**  ~~Tea.~~ *Tea, please.*

**Lina**   With milk?

**Jason**  Yes.

**Lina**   Sugar?

**Jason**  No.

**Lina**   And a biscuit?

**Jason**  Biscuit?

**Lina**   A biscuit is a cookie.

**Jason**  Oh, a cookie. Sure, please.

## 1 READING

A Read about vacation home-shares. Is each home good for two people or for a family (parents + two or three children)? Check (✓) the box.

1 ☐ Two people ☐ Family

**$65, center of Rio de Janeiro**

This is a great apartment for one or two weeks. The bedroom is small, but the bed is big. The couch in the living room is a good bed for a child. The living room has a big bookcase and cool pictures on the walls. It has interesting books about Brazil. The kitchen is big and has a table and four chairs. The apartment is a great place to stay. – MATT

2 ☐ Two people ☐ Family

**$110, Lapa, Rio de Janeiro**

This home is in Lapa, in Rio de Janeiro. The bedrooms in the home are great. One bedroom is big and has a big bed. The second bedroom has two beds. The third bedroom is small and has a small bed. It's good for a child. The apartment has two bathrooms! The showers are great. The kitchen is nice, but the refrigerator is small. It's a good place for four or five days. – KARA

B Read about the homes again. Check (✓) the things in the homes.

| | | Center of Rio de Janeiro | Lapa, Rio de Janeiro |
|---|---|---|---|
| 1 | bathroom | | |
| 2 | bedroom | | |
| 3 | dining area | | |
| 4 | kitchen | | |
| 5 | living room | | |
| 6 | bookcase | | |
| 7 | desk | | |
| 8 | picture | | |
| 9 | shower | | |
| 10 | television | | |

## 2 GRAMMAR: Information questions with *be*

A Match the question words and answers.

1 What? _____     a six years old
2 Where? _____     b five
3 How old? _____     c Maria Santos
4 Who? _____     d Rio de Janeiro
5 How many rooms? _____     e myb@xyzmail.com

B  **Write the questions and answers from exercise 2A.**

1  (your email address)     A  What is your email address?
                            B  It's myb@xyzmail.com

2  (the apartment)          A  _____
                            B  _____

3  (old/apartment)          A  _____
                            B  _____

4  (owner)                  A  _____
                            B  _____

5  (rooms)                  A  _____
                            B  _____

## 3  WRITING

A  **Underline** the **five** questions in the email. Change the periods to question marks.

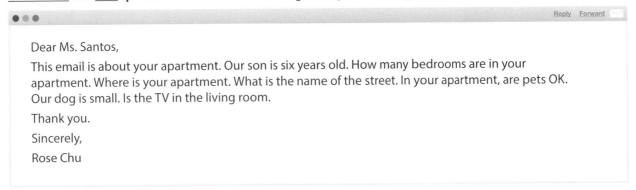

Reply  Forward

Dear Ms. Santos,

This email is about your apartment. Our son is six years old. How many bedrooms are in your apartment. Where is your apartment. What is the name of the street. In your apartment, are pets OK. Our dog is small. Is the TV in the living room.

Thank you.

Sincerely,

Rose Chu

B  **Is the email in exercise 3A formal or informal?**

C  **You go to a new city for one week. Write an email to the owner of a home-share. Ask questions.**

# CHECK AND REVIEW

**Read the statements. Can you do these things?**

| UNIT 3 | Mark the boxes. ✔ I can do it. ? I am not sure.  I can … | If you are not sure, go back to these pages in the Student's Book. |
|---|---|---|
| VOCABULARY | ☐ use words for rooms in my home. | page 22 |
| | ☐ use words for furniture. | page 24 |
| | ☐ use words for drinks and snacks. | page 26 |
| GRAMMAR | ☐ use possessive adjectives, 's, and s'. | page 23 |
| | ☐ use *it is*. | page 25 |
| | ☐ ask questions with *be* for information. | page 28 |
| FUNCTIONAL LANGUAGE | ☐ make and reply to offers. | page 26 |
| | ☐ ask about words I don't understand. | page 27 |
| SKILLS | ☐ write an email about a vacation home. | page 29 |
| | ☐ use question marks. | page 29 |

# UNIT 4    I LOVE IT

## 4.1    FAVORITE THINGS

### 1    VOCABULARY: Technology

A    **Find the words in the box in the word search.**

| app | camera | ~~cell phone~~ | earphones |
|-----|--------|-----------|-----------|
| game | laptop | tablet | smartwatch |

| L | A | P | T | O | P | T | D | W | Z | T |
|---|---|---|---|---|---|---|---|---|---|---|
| Z | N | B | C | J | G | A | M | E | Q | A |
| J | K | Y | A | C | K | E | I | K | B | B |
| M | G | V | M | A | T | Z | I | K | H | L |
| R | Y | C | E | L | L | P | H | O | N | E |
| K | E | O | R | T | O | P | Z | A | M | T |
| A | P | L | A | S | E | T | Y | T | N | P |
| E | E | A | R | P | H | O | N | E | S | X |
| A | P | P | M | F | S | Z | N | R | V | K |
| F | S | M | A | R | T | W | A | T | C | H |

B    **Write the correct word to match each picture. Use the words in the box in exercise 1A.**

1 _____

2 _____

3 _____cell phone_____

4 _____

5 _____

6 _____

7 _____

8 _____

### 2    GRAMMAR: Simple present statements with *I*, *you*, and *we*

A    **Write affirmative (+) and negative (–) statements.**

1    I / not have / a laptop // have / a tablet

   _I don't have a laptop. I have a tablet._

2    I like apps // not like / video games

3    you / want / a small refrigerator

   // not want / a big refrigerator

4    I / love / photo apps // not love / music apps

5    we / have / an apartment // not have / a house

6    we / not want / a new camera // want / a new computer

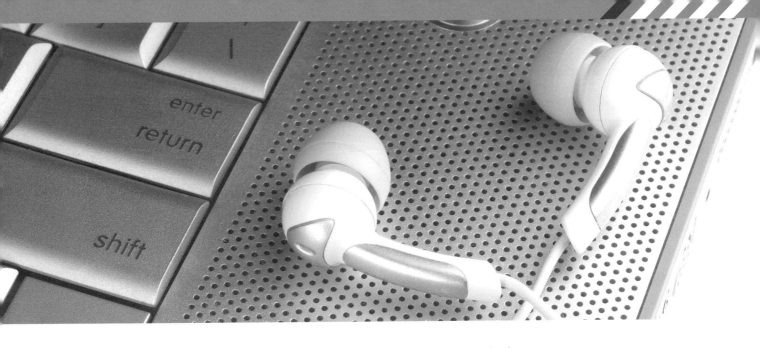

**B** Write affirmative (+) and negative (−) sentences. Use the verbs in the box.
Start the sentences with *I* or *We.*

| have | like | love | want |
|------|------|------|------|

1   We have a new apartment. We don't have a new couch.

2   _____

3   _____

4   _____

5   _____

## 3  GRAMMAR AND VOCABULARY

**A**   **Write sentences that are true for you. Then add more information.**

1   love video games

   I love video games. I have games on my phone.

   OR

   I don't love video games. I don't have games on my phone.

2   have cool apps on my phone

   _____

3   like earphones

   _____

4   want a new tablet

   _____

5   have an old laptop

   _____

6   love my cell phone

   _____

7   want a smartwatch

   _____

8   like the camera on my phone

   _____

# 4.2 MY PHONE IS MY WORLD

## 1 VOCABULARY: Using technology

A Look at the verbs (1–10). Which <u>two</u> words go after each verb? (Circle) the correct answers.

| | | | | | | |
|---|---|---|---|---|---|---|
| 1 | call | **a** a game | **(b)** a company | **c** my cousin |
| 2 | chat with | **a** my best friend | **b** my couch | **c** my sister |
| 3 | listen to | **a** my desk | **b** music | **c** my teacher |
| 4 | post | **a** apps | **b** messages | **c** photos |
| 5 | read | **a** an email | **b** a photo | **c** a text |
| 6 | send | **a** an email | **b** a photo | **c** social media |
| 7 | leave | **a** a message | **b** a comment | **c** an app |
| 8 | use | **a** my music | **b** my computer | **c** my watch |
| 9 | watch | **a** a comment | **b** a movie | **c** a video |
| 10 | buy | **a** my family | **b** apps | **c** a cell phone |

B Look at 1–6. Write *on*, or write *X* where *on* is not correct.

1 _____ the internet       4 _____ the tablet
2 _____ my phone          5 _____ my laptop
3 _____ my room           6 _____ China

## 2 GRAMMAR: Simple present *yes/no* questions with *I, you, we*

A Complete the questions with the verbs.

1 _____*Do you have*_____ a laptop? (you/have)
2 _____ social media apps? (you and your friends/love)
3 _____ your family? (you/call)
4 _____ photos on social media? (I/post)
5 _____ a new tablet? (you and your family want)
6 _____ videos on the internet? (you/watch)

B Answer the questions in exercise 2A so they are true for you.

1 _____Yes, I do. OR No, I don't._____
2 _____
3 _____
4 _____
5 _____
6 _____

28

## 3 GRAMMAR AND VOCABULARY

**A** **Complete the sentences so they are true for you.**

1  I use my _____ *laptop* _____ at school.
2  I chat with _____ on my phone.
3  I call my _____ on my tablet.
4  We watch _____ on my laptop at home.
5  I don't post _____ .
6  I read _____ on the internet.
7  My friends and I send _____ .
8  I leave messages for my _____ .
9  I listen to _____ on my phone.
10  I don't play _____ .

**B** **Read the words and then write questions and answers that are true for you.**

1  social media
   *Do you post comments on social media?* _____   Yes, I do. OR No, I don't. _____

2  chat on your phone
   _____   _____

3  watch videos on TV
   _____   _____

4  send emails
   _____   _____

5  leave voice messages
   _____   _____

6  call your friends
   _____   _____

# 4.3 WHAT ABOUT YOU?

## 1 FUNCTIONAL LANGUAGE: Continuing a conversation

**A** **Put the conversation in the correct order.**

| | | |
|---|---|---|
| **Juan** | Yes, and I send thank-you emails to my friends. | ___ |
| **David** | No. I use email or social media. | ___ |
| **Juan** | Do you send text messages to your parents? | 1 |
| **David** | Do you send thank-you cards, too? | ___ |
| **David** | Yeah, I send birthday cards to my grandparents. How about you? | ___ |
| **Juan** | What about cards? | ___ |
| **Juan** | Yes, I send cards, too. I like cards with interesting pictures. | ___ |

## 2 REAL-WORLD STRATEGY: Showing you are listening

**A** Circle **the best response to complete the conversations.**

1  A  I love Instagram.
   B  *Yeah, me too. / How about you?*
   A  It's really cool.

2  A  Do you use Snapchat?
   B  *Right. / No. How about you?*
   A  I love it.

3  A  I use video chat a lot. What about you?
   B  *Yeah. / OK.*
   A  I like video chat.

4  A  This is a great new app!
   B  *Right. / No.*
   A  I really like it.

5  A  I buy music on the internet.
   B  *Yeah. / I like email.*
   A  It's good.

6  A  Do you watch movies on your cell phone?
   B  *No, I don't. / Right.*
   A  I do. It's great.

## 3 FUNCTIONAL LANGUAGE AND REAL-WORLD STRATEGY

**A** **Complete the sentences. Follow the instructions in parentheses ( ).**

**Ana**  I don't call my family on my cell phone.

**Sam**  Really?

**Ana**  Yeah, it's expensive.

**Sam**  Yes, it is. [1]Do you use video chat? _____ (*Ask a question to start a new topic.*)

**Ana**  Sorry, I don't understand. What is a video chat?

**Sam**  You talk with your friends with video. I use video chat on the internet. It's free.

**Ana**  [2] _____ (*Show Ana is listening.*)

**Sam**  We have an app.

**Ana**  [3] _____ Is Skype an app for video chats?
(*Show Ana is listening.*)

**Sam**  Yes, it's one app. I use WhatsApp, too.

**Ana**  [4] _____ (*Ask a question to start a new topic.*)

**Sam**  I don't use email. I send texts.

**Ana**  [5] _____ (*Ask for a response about the topic.*)

**Sam**  Oh, no. I don't text my family. I call them. [6] _____
(*Ask for a response about the topic.*)

**Ana**  I send emails to my parents. They don't like texts.

**Sam**  Really?

31

# 4.4 GREAT! FIVE STARS

## 1 LISTENING

A 🔊 **4.01** **LISTEN FOR DETAILS** What do Mai and Jonas talk about? (Circle) the correct answer.

1 video games
2 apps
3 product reviews
4 their favorite things

B 🔊 **4.01** **LISTEN FOR SUPPORTING DETAILS** Listen again. Check (✓) what Mai and Jonas say about their phones.

|  | Mai | Jonas |
|---|---|---|
| 1 loves the phone | ✔ | |
| 2 doesn't like the phone | | |
| 3 has great apps | | |
| 4 reads email | | |
| 5 sends text messages | | |
| 6 posts comments on social media | | |
| 7 doesn't like the music app | | |

## 2 GRAMMAR: *a/an*; Adjectives before nouns

A (Circle) *a* or *an* in each sentence.

1 We don't have *a* / *(an)* apartment.
2 We have *a* / *an* house.
3 She has *a* / *an* app for video chat.
4 You don't have *a* / *an* email address.
5 He doesn't use *a* / *an* tablet.

B **Make one long sentence from the two short sentences.**

1 It's a book. It's interesting.  *It's an interesting book.*
2 I have a TV. It's expensive.
3 It's a card. It's great.
4 Are they games? Are they boring?
5 It's a movie. It's old.
6 It's a smartwatch. It's cool.

## 3 WRITING

**A** Match the beginning of the sentence (1–6) with the end of the sentence (a–f).

1 I like to listen to music, but _____     **a** my friends use it.
2 I don't like social media, but _____     **b** it's old.
3 I don't have a smartwatch because ___f___     **c** I don't like earphones.
4 We watch videos on the laptop, but _____     **d** it takes good pictures.
5 I don't use my laptop because _____     **e** we want a new TV.
6 We like the camera because _____     **f** they're really expensive.

**B** Read the thank-you email. Add two exclamation points.

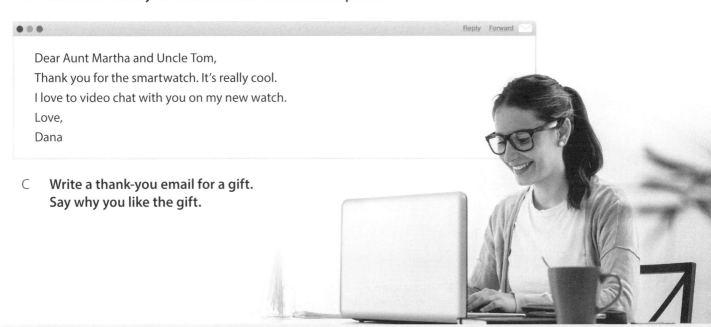

Reply  Forward

Dear Aunt Martha and Uncle Tom,
Thank you for the smartwatch. It's really cool.
I love to video chat with you on my new watch.
Love,
Dana

**C** Write a thank-you email for a gift.
Say why you like the gift.

# CHECK AND REVIEW

Read the statements. Can you do these things?

| UNIT 4 | Mark the boxes. ☑ I can do it. ? I am not sure.<br>I can … | If you are not sure, go back to these pages in the Student's Book. |
|---|---|---|
| VOCABULARY | ☐ use technology words.<br>☐ use verbs for using technology.<br>☐ use *on* before certain words. | page 34<br>page 36<br>page 36 |
| GRAMMAR | ☐ use the simple present with *I*, *you*, and *we*.<br>☐ use *yes/no* questions in the simple present with *I*, *you*, and *we*.<br>☐ use *a/an* and adjectives before nouns. | page 35<br>page 37<br><br>page 40 |
| FUNCTIONAL LANGUAGE | ☐ ask questions to develop a conversation.<br>☐ show I am listening. | page 38<br>page 39 |
| SKILLS | ☐ write a thank-you email.<br>☐ use exclamation points. | page 41<br>page 41 |

## 5.1 PLAY OR FAST-FORWARD?

### 1 VOCABULARY: Days and times of day; everyday activities

A **Look at the words in the box. Write the words.**

| ~~in the morning~~ | ~~on Saturday~~ | play soccer | work | on Wednesday | run |
|---|---|---|---|---|---|
| go out | on Thursday | in the evening | on Friday | at night | |
| in the afternoon | on Monday | on Tuesday | study | on Sunday | |

| | | | | | |
|---|---|---|---|---|---|
| **Activities** | | | | | |
| **Days of the week** | on Saturday | | | | |
| **Times** | in the morning | | | | |

B **Read about Rhea and Jon. Complete the sentences.**

| | Monday | Tuesday | Wednesday | Thursday | Friday | Saturday | Sunday |
|---|---|---|---|---|---|---|---|
| **Rhea** | morning: work | morning: work | morning: work<br><br>evening: go out with Teri and Jon | morning: work | morning: work<br><br>night: go out with Jon | morning: run with Jay | afternoon: go out with family |
| **Jon** | morning: study<br><br>evening: work | morning: study<br><br>evening: work | morning: study<br><br>evening: go out with Teri and Rhea | morning: study<br><br>evening: work | morning: work<br><br>night: go out with Rhea | morning: play soccer | morning: play soccer |

1 Rhea works <u>in the morning from Monday to Friday</u> .

2 On Saturday, Rhea _____ .

3 On Wednesday evening, Rhea _____ .

4 Rhea _____ with her family _____ .

5 Jon _____ in the morning from Monday to Thursday.

6 On the weekend, Jon _____ .

7 Jon works _____ .

8 On Friday night _____ .

### 2 GRAMMAR: Simple present statements with *he, she* and *they*

A **Complete the sentences with affirmative (+) verbs.**

1 Javier and Allie play soccer on Friday. Allie _____plays_____ on Saturday, too.

2 Maddie and Nat go to class on Monday night. Alma _____ on Wednesday night.

3 Jay, Laura, and Terry have fun on weekends. Their brother _____ fun on weekdays.

**4** My wife wants a refrigerator. My children _____ a TV.

**5** My friends and I study before class. Hugo _____ after work.

**6** Miranda works in the morning. Eric and Alan _____ in the afternoon.

B **Complete the sentences with negative (–) verbs.**

**1** I don't study in the morning. My friends _____*don't study*_____ at night.

**2** Juliana and Roberta don't have free time on Friday. Max _____ free time on Thursday.

**3** Robin doesn't run in the morning. Her friends _____ in the afternoon.

**4** Mr. and Mrs. Cho don't go out on the weekend. Their son _____ out on weekdays.

**5** I don't watch TV. My cousin _____ videos.

**6** Chen and Juan don't like coffee. Sam _____ tea.

C **Read the words. Then make correct sentences.**

**1** ☐ my laptop. / use / never / I _____*I never use my laptop.*_____

**2** ☐ and / hardly ever / soccer. / my friends / I / play _____

**3** ☐ My sister / at / studies / usually / night. _____

**4** ☐ go out / I / night. / Friday / often / on _____

**5** ☐ at / on / always / are / the weekend. / They / home _____

## 3 GRAMMAR AND VOCABULARY

A **Complete the sentences about what you do and don't do in the week. Make them true for you.**

**1** I always _____*sleep in the morning*_____ on the weekends.

**2** I usually _____ in the evening.

**3** I often _____ in the morning.

**4** I sometimes _____ on Monday afternoon.

**5** I hardly ever _____ on Sunday.

**6** I never _____.

B **Read about what Katya and Lucas do. Then write five affirmative (+) and negative (–) sentences.**

|  | Katya | Lucas |
|---|---|---|
| go out on Friday night | never | usually |
| have fun on weekends | often | never |
| play soccer | never | hardly ever |
| watch soccer games on Saturday | sometimes | never |
| run early in the morning | usually | usually |
| study at night | usually | never |
| study in the morning | hardly ever | usually |
| work on Saturday and Sunday | never | always |
| work on Friday night | always | never |

**1** _____*Katya doesn't go out on Friday night. She always works on Friday night.*_____

**2** _____

**3** _____

**4** _____

**5** _____

**6** _____

## 1 VOCABULARY: Telling the time

A  **Look at the pictures and write the times.**

1 _____It's two thirty._____   2 _____   3 _____

4 _____   5 _____   6 _____

B  **Put the sentences in order for you. Then write the times for you. Write *X* for activities you do not do.**

| | | |
|---|---|---|
| _____ | I drink coffee | ........................................... |
| _____ | I go to class | ........................................... |
| _____ | I go to work | ........................................... |
| _____ | I eat breakfast | ........................................... |
| 1 | I get up | *at 7:00 a.m.* |
| _____ | I go to bed | ........................................... |
| _____ | I drink tea | ........................................... |
| _____ | I have dinner | ........................................... |
| _____ | I eat lunch | ........................................... |

## 2 GRAMMAR: Simple present questions

A  **Read the answers. Then complete the *yes/no* questions and information questions.**

1  A  _____Does_____ your family _____have_____ a big lunch on Saturday?
   B  No, my family doesn't have a big lunch on Saturday.
   A  _____What does_____ your family have on Saturday?
   B  They have a big breakfast on Saturday.

2  A  _____ you _____ late on Monday?
   B  No, I don't get up late on Monday.
   A  _____ you get up late?
   B  I get up late on Sunday.

3  A  _____ your best friend _____ basketball?
   B  No, he doesn't play basketball.
   A  _____ your best friend play?
   B  He plays soccer.

**4  A** _____ your teacher _____ on weekends?

**B** No, she doesn't work on weekends.

**A** _____ your teacher work?

**B** She works from Monday to Friday.

**5  A** _____ you _____ lunch at school?

**B** No, I don't eat lunch at school.

**A** _____ you eat lunch?

**B** I eat lunch at home.

**6  A** _____ your friends _____ to bed late on Friday and Saturday?

**B** Yes, they go to bed late on Friday and Saturday.

**A** _____ your friends go to bed on Friday and Saturday?

**B** They go to bed after midnight.

**B**   **Look at the *yes/no* questions in exercise 2A. Write true answers.**

1  _Yes, we do._ OR No, we don't.      4  _____

2  _____                     5  _____

3  _____                     6  _____

## 3 GRAMMAR AND VOCABULARY

**A**   **Write six questions. Use each word in column A.**

| A | B | C |
|---|---|---|
| What<br>What time<br>When<br>Where<br>Do<br>Does | you<br>your parents<br>your mother<br>your father<br>your brother(s) and sister(s)<br>your brother(s)<br>your sister(s)<br>your best friend<br>your friends<br>your teacher | do on weekends<br>drink coffee / tea<br>eat breakfast / lunch / dinner<br>get up<br>go to bed / classes / work<br>go out<br>have breakfast / lunch / dinner<br>have fun<br>play basketball / games / soccer<br>study<br>work |

1  _Do your parents go out on the weekend?_ OR _When do your parents go out?_

2  _____

3  _____

4  _____

5  _____

6  _____

7  _____

**B**   **Answer the questions in exercise 3A for you.**

1  Do your parents go out on the weekend?  _No, they don't._

When do your parents go out?  _They go out on their birthdays._

# 5.3 ME, TOO

## 1 FUNCTIONAL LANGUAGE: Showing you agree and have things in common

A Circle the correct responses.

1 You study a lot.
   a Yeah, I know.
   b Me, neither.
   c Me, too.

2 Sports are great.
   a Yeah, I know. They are boring.
   b That's true. I hardly ever watch them.
   c I agree. I play a lot of sports.

3 A good job is important.
   a I agree. What about you?
   b That's true.
   c Me, too.

4 I don't work on weekends.
   a Me, neither. But I work on Friday.
   b Me, too. I work on Saturday morning.
   c I agree. I don't work on weekends.

B Val and Mateo have a lot in common. Complete Mateo's sentences with *Me, too* or *Me, neither*.

| | | | | |
|---|---|---|---|---|
| 1 | **Val** | I love my phone. | **Mateo** | *Me, too.* |
| 2 | **Val** | I don't get up early on weekends. | **Mateo** | |
| 3 | **Val** | I don't eat a big breakfast. | **Mateo** | |
| 4 | **Val** | I run in the evening. | **Mateo** | |
| 5 | **Val** | I go to bed late. | **Mateo** | |
| 6 | **Val** | I don't drink tea. | **Mateo** | |

## 2 REAL-WORLD STRATEGY: Short answers with adverbs of frequency

A Answer the questions for you. Use adverbs of frequency.

1 A Do you run?
  B   *Sometimes.*

2 A Do you eat breakfast?
  B

3 A Do you go out on weekends?
  B

4 A Do you study in the morning?
  B

5 A Do you go to bed at 10 o'clock?
  B

6 A Do you play video games?
  B

## 3 FUNCTIONAL LANGUAGE AND REAL-WORLD STRATEGY

A   **Complete the conversation. Use the words in the box.**

| | | | |
|---|---|---|---|
| agree | ~~do~~ | hardly ever | neither |
| sometimes | too | true | yeah |

**Min-seo**  ¹_____Do_____ you watch TV on the weekend?

**David**  ²_____. I think it's boring.

**Min-seo**  I ³_____. I only watch sports on TV.

**David**  What sports do you watch?

**Min-seo**  All sports. I love sports.

**David**  Me, ⁴_____.

**Min-seo**  Do you play sports?

**David**  No. I don't have a lot of free time.

**Min-seo**  Me, ⁵_____.

**David**  But I run every day before dinner. Exercise is good.

**Min-seo**  That's ⁶_____.

**David**  How about you? Do you run?

**Min-seo**  ⁷_____. My friends and I run on the beach on the weekend.

**David**  The beach is a great place to run.

**Min-seo**  ⁸_____, I know.

B   **You meet a new person. You have a lot in common. Write a conversation. Ask about their free time activities. Use adverbs of frequency and words from the box in exercise 3A.**

_____

_____

_____

_____

_____

_____

_____

_____

_____

_____

_____

_____

_____

# 5.4 A HAPPY LIFE

## 1 READING

A **SKIM** Skim the magazine article. Then check (✓) the correct title.

| | | |
|---|---|---|
| _____ | **Title One:** | All Play and No Work Is Not Good for Children |
| _____ | **Title Two:** | All Work and No Play Is Not Good for Children |
| _____ | **Title Three:** | All Sleep and No Play Is Not Good for Children |

Eva is 12 years old. She gets up at 6:00 a.m. and studies for an hour before breakfast. She goes to school at 8:30 and comes home after 6 o'clock. She eats lunch at school and studies for an hour before her afternoon classes. After school on Monday, she has guitar lessons. After school on Tuesday and Thursday, she has Chinese class. After dinner, she plays the guitar and studies from 7:00 to 10:30. She usually goes to bed at 11:00 p.m.

What does Eva do on weekends? Does she have fun? She gets up at 8:00 or 8:30. But after breakfast, she plays the guitar from 10 a.m. to 1 p.m. Then she eats lunch and reads a book. She doesn't have time for fun on the weekends! She goes to bed early – she's _always_ tired!

Eva's a very good student, but is she happy? Are children happy when they don't play? Doctors say "no." Many children study in the evenings and on the weekends. This isn't good and the children aren't happy. Children want free time! Doctors tell parents: "Make sure your children work AND play!"

B **READ FOR DETAIL** Read again. Complete the chart with three of Eva's weekday activities and the times for morning, afternoon, and evening/night.

| Morning activities | Afternoon activities | Evening/Night activities |
|---|---|---|
| 1 _She gets up at 6:00 a.m._ | 1 _____ | 1 _____ |
| 2 _____ | 2 _____ | 2 _____ |
| 3 _____ | 3 _____ | 3 _____ |

## 2 LISTENING

A 🔊 **5.01** **LISTEN FOR SUPPORTING DETAILS** Listen to the conversation. Write the numbers in the sentences.

1 Dave: "I have _____one/1_____ chocolate cookie before I go to bed."

2 Dave sleeps four or _____ hours a night.

3 He drinks _____ cups of coffee a day.

4 He eats _____ meals a day.

5 He runs _____ days a week.

6 He works at his desk _____ or _____ hours a day.

40

## 3 WRITING

A Read the headings (1–3) in the report. Use the sentences about Dave in exercise 2A to complete sentences a–f.

B **REGISTER CHECK** Write the sentences without *a.m.* or *p.m.*

1 We play basketball at 7 p.m.
   *We play basketball at seven in the evening.*

2 I go to class at 8 a.m.

3 I study at 1 p.m.

4 I run at 6 a.m.

5 I go to bed at 11:30 p.m.

## The "Good for You" Report

**1** Great for you

a _____

b _____

**2** Not good, but not bad for you

c  I have one chocolate cookie before I go to bed.

d _____

**3** Really bad for you

e _____

f _____

SCORE:

★★★★★

C Write your routines in the chart and make a "Good for You" report. Put a score at the end.

| Great for you | Not good, but not bad for you | Really bad for you |
|---|---|---|
|  |  |  |

SCORE
★★★★★

# CHECK AND REVIEW

Read the statements. Can you do these things?

| UNIT 5 | Mark the boxes.  ☑ I can do it.  ☐? I am not sure.<br>I can … | If you are not sure, go back to these pages in the Student's Book. |
|---|---|---|
| VOCABULARY | ☐ say days of the week and times of day.<br>☐ tell the time.<br>☐ use words for activities and routines. | page 44<br>page 46<br>pages 44 and 46 |
| GRAMMAR | ☐ use the simple present with *he/she/they*.<br>☐ ask *yes/no* and information questions in the simple present. | page 45<br>page 47 |
| FUNCTIONAL LANGUAGE | ☐ show I agree or have things in common with someone.<br>☐ answer questions with adverbs of frequency. | page 48<br>page 49 |
| SKILLS | ☐ write a report. | page 51 |

## 1 VOCABULARY: Places in cities

A **Match the sentences (1–14) with the places (a–n).**

| | | | | |
|---|---|---|---|---|
| 1 | "I like animals." | n | **a** | bookstore |
| 2 | "I want a new book." | | **b** | café |
| 3 | "I'm a doctor." | | **c** | college |
| 4 | "I love movies." | | **d** | hospital |
| 5 | "I'm a student, and I'm 20 years old." | | **e** | hotel |
| 6 | "I'm a student, and I'm 12 years old." | | **f** | mall |
| 7 | "I'm from the United States. I'm in Lima for five days." | | **g** | movie theater |
| 8 | "I love pictures by great artists." | | **h** | museum |
| 9 | "I want an expensive dinner." | | **i** | park |
| 10 | "I want coffee and a cookie." | | **j** | restaurant |
| 11 | "My children play with their friends after school." | | **k** | school |
| 12 | "I don't have milk or sugar at home." | | **l** | store |
| 13 | "I want some earphones, a camera, and tea." | | **m** | supermarket |
| 14 | "I want new furniture." | | **n** | zoo |

## 2 GRAMMAR: *There's, There are; a lot of, some, no*

A **Complete the sentences about Amy's apartment. Use *there's* or *there are*.**

I live in a small town. In our town [1] _____there's_____ a big park, but [2] _____ no zoo.
[3] _____ a big supermarket, too, and [4] _____ three stores. My daughter goes to the
school and my husband is a teacher at the school. [5] _____ an interesting bookstore.
[6] _____ two really good restaurants!

B **Complete the conversation about Don's hotel. Use** *no, a, some,* **or** *a lot of.*

**Clara**  Do you like your hotel, Don?

**Don**  Yes, I do. It's a big hotel! There are [1] _____ rooms.

**Clara**  Does the hotel have a restaurant?

**Don**  Yes, it has [2] _____ big restaurant. I eat breakfast in the restaurant every day.

**Clara**  What about the restaurants near the hotel? Are they good?

**Don**  Yes. There are [3] _____ great restaurants near the hotel. Italian, Japanese, Spanish …

**Clara**  And is your room good?

**Don**  It's OK. There's [4] _____ desk, [5] _____ chair, and [6] _____ big TV, but there's [7] _____ sofa. It's not good!

## 3 GRAMMAR AND VOCABULARY

A **Write sentences about Ramón's city. Use** *there's, there are, a, no, some,* **and** *a lot of.*

| | |
|---|---|
| 8 parks | 2,000,000 people |
| 3 hospitals | 0 movie theaters |
| 5 cafés | 20 restaurants |
| 1 hotel | 0 good restaurants |

1  There are a lot of parks.          5  _____

2  _____          6  _____

3  _____          7  _____

4  _____          8  _____

B **Write six sentences about things you like and don't like about your city.**
**Use** *there's, there are, a, no, some,* **and** *a lot of.*

1  _____

2  _____

3  _____

4  _____

5  _____

6  _____

## 1 VOCABULARY: Nature

A **Look at the pictures and check (✓) the correct box.**

1 ☑ island, lake, snow
  ☐ river, flowers, hills
  ☐ forest, beach, mountains

3 ☐ desert, snow, forest
  ☐ forest, river, mountains
  ☐ hills, plants, flowers

2 ☐ island, grass, trees
  ☐ hills, plants, lake
  ☐ beach, flowers, ocean

4 ☐ plants, desert, mountains
  ☐ snow, trees, hills
  ☐ beach, grass, island

## 2 GRAMMAR: Count and non-count nouns

A **Circle the five mistakes.**

| Count nouns | Non-count nouns |
| --- | --- |
| apartment | (animal) |
| artist | coffee |
| grass | furniture |
| milk | house |
| refrigerator | nature |
| restaurant | plant |
| sugar | snow |

B **Complete the sentences. Use *a*, *an*, or *some*.**

1  I am _____*an*_____ artist.
2  I have _____ house in a small city.
3  I don't have _____ large apartment.
4  There's _____ grass in my garden.
5  There's _____ table in the dining area.
6  There's _____ furniture in the house.
7  There's _____ plant in the living room.
8  There's _____ refrigerator in the kitchen.
9  There's _____ milk in the refrigerator.
10  There's _____ coffee next to the refrigerator.

## 3  GRAMMAR AND VOCABULARY

A  **Complete the sentences. Use *There's* or *There are* and *a* or *a lot of*.**

1  ___*There are*___  ___*a lot of*___ hills in my city.
2  _____ _____ very tall tree.
3  _____ _____ grass.
4  _____ _____ flowers.
5  _____ _____ lake.
6  _____ _____ plants.
7  _____ _____ mountain.
8  _____ _____ snow on the mountain.

B  **Look out your window. What do you see? Write <u>six</u> sentences. Use *There is* or *There are*. Use *a*, *an*, *no*, *some*, or *a lot of*.**

# 6.3 IS IT NEAR HERE?

## 1 FUNCTIONAL LANGUAGE: Asking for and giving directions

A **Complete the conversation. Use the words in the box.**

> block     near     this     turn right     ~~where's~~

**Marina** Excuse me. [1] _Where's_ Central Hospital?

**Ricky** It's on Milk Street.

**Marina** Is [2] _____ Milk Street?

**Ricky** No, it isn't. This is Garden Street.

**Marina** Is Milk Street [3] _____ here?

**Ricky** Yes, it is. Turn left here. Then [4] _____ on Park Street. Go one [5] _____ .
The hospital is on the left.

## 2 REAL-WORLD STRATEGY: Checking information

A **Complete the conversation.**

**Martin** Excuse me. Where's the supermarket?

**Althea** Go one block and turn right on Good Street.

**Martin** [1] _So, go one block and turn right on Good Street._

**Althea** Yes. Turn right on Good Street. [2] _____

**Martin** So, after the bookstore, turn right again.

**Althea** Yes. That's Second Street. Go two blocks and turn left.

**Martin** [3] _____

**Althea** That's right. That's Market Street. [4] _____

**Martin** So, the supermarket is on Market Street, on the right.

**Althea** Yes.

46

## 3 FUNCTIONAL LANGUAGE AND REAL-WORLD STRATEGY

A   **Look at the map and read the conversation. Complete the directions.**

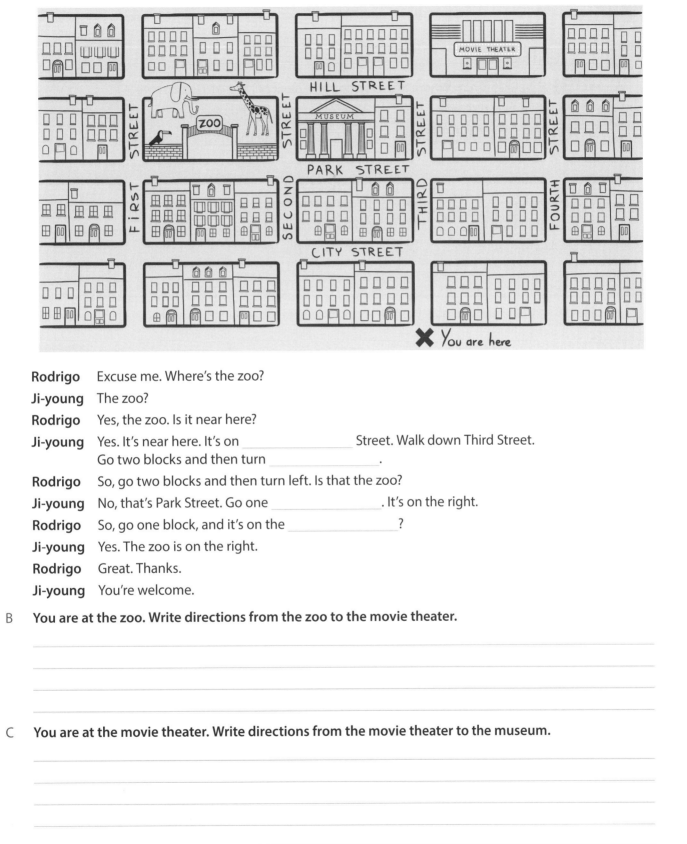

**Rodrigo**   Excuse me. Where's the zoo?

**Ji-young**   The zoo?

**Rodrigo**   Yes, the zoo. Is it near here?

**Ji-young**   Yes. It's near here. It's on _____ Street. Walk down Third Street. Go two blocks and then turn _____ .

**Rodrigo**   So, go two blocks and then turn left. Is that the zoo?

**Ji-young**   No, that's Park Street. Go one _____ . It's on the right.

**Rodrigo**   So, go one block, and it's on the _____ ?

**Ji-young**   Yes. The zoo is on the right.

**Rodrigo**   Great. Thanks.

**Ji-young**   You're welcome.

B   **You are at the zoo. Write directions from the zoo to the movie theater.**

_____

_____

_____

_____

C   **You are at the movie theater. Write directions from the movie theater to the museum.**

_____

_____

_____

_____

_____

# A FOREST IN THE CITY

## 1 LISTENING

A 🔊 6.01 **LISTEN FOR GIST** Where are the people? Check (✓) the correct answer.

_____ in a movie theater    _____ in a car    _____ in a house

B 🔊 6.01 **LISTEN FOR EXAMPLES** Listen again. Check (✓) the things the people see.

1 ☑ a building
2 ☐ a garden
3 ☐ a park
4 ☐ a green building
5 ☐ a garden on a wall

6 ☐ plants on a wall
7 ☐ flowers on a wall
8 ☐ trees on a wall
9 ☐ animals on a wall
10 ☐ grass on a wall

## 2 READING

A Read the article and the questions. Are the answers to the questions in the article? Check (✓) *Yes* or *No*.

# What are vertical gardens?

They are gardens on walls. Vertical gardens are on tall buildings and on short buildings, and they are inside buildings and outside buildings. These gardens have a lot of different plants. Some vertical gardens have 400 different plants! Vertical gardens are good for cities and they are good for people. There are vertical gardens in many cities in the world. Sydney, Singapore, and Mexico City have vertical gardens. What about *your* city? Does it have a vertical garden?

|   |   | Yes | No |
|---|---|-----|-----|
| 1 | What is a vertical garden? | ☐ | ☐ |
| 2 | Who makes vertical gardens? | ☐ | ☐ |
| 3 | Is a vertical garden expensive? | ☐ | ☐ |
| 4 | Are gardens good for people? | ☐ | ☐ |
| 5 | What are the names of some cities with vertical gardens? | ☐ | ☐ |

## 3 WRITING

**A** Read the words and make sentences.

1 nice / have / parks / some / we / small      *We have some nice small parks.*

2 there / beautiful / trees / some / tall / are

3 of / are / lot / flowers / small / interesting / there / a

4 plants / big / are / there / a / of / nice / lot

5 tall / the / has / trees / great / some / park

**B** Read the fact sheet and add *very* to make the adjectives strong.

> Via Verde is a busy road in Mexico City.
> There are 30 kilometers of vertical gardens next to the road.
> Via Verde is a big vertical garden. There are 700 small gardens in it.
> There are a lot of interesting plants in the gardens.
> People like the plants and flowers on Via Verde.
> People in Mexico City think the vertical gardens are interesting.
> Vertical gardens are important to Mexico City.

**C** Write a fact sheet about an interesting place you know. Use *very*. Do <u>not</u> use contractions.

# CHECK AND REVIEW

Read the statements. Can you do these things?

| UNIT 6 | Mark the boxes.   ☑ I can do it.   ? I am not sure.<br>I can … | If you are not sure, go back to these pages in the Student's Book. |
|---|---|---|
| VOCABULARY | ☐ use words for places in cities.<br>☐ use words for places in nature. | page 54<br>page 56 |
| GRAMMAR | ☐ use *There's/There are* with *a/an, some, a lot of, no*.<br>☐ use count and non-count nouns. | page 55<br>page 57 |
| FUNCTIONAL LANGUAGE | ☐ ask for and give directions.<br>☐ check information by repeating. | page 58<br>page 59 |
| SKILLS | ☐ write a fact sheet.<br>☐ use *very* correctly. | page 61<br>page 61 |

## 7.1 A GOOD TIME TO CALL

### 1 VOCABULARY: Activities around the house

A **Cross out the words that do <u>not</u> complete the sentences.**

| | | | | |
|---|---|---|---|---|
| 1 | I clean _____ on the weekend. | the bathroom | the kitchen | ~~my hair~~ |
| 2 | We cook _____ every day. | coffee | dinner | breakfast |
| 3 | He washes _____ at night. | the computer | his hair | the dog |
| 4 | She brushes _____ in the morning. | her hair | her bed | her teeth |
| 5 | I take _____ every morning. | a bath | my room | a shower |
| 6 | They do _____ in the evening. | their breakfast | the dishes | their homework |
| 7 | You help _____ a lot. | your friends | your home | your mother |

### 2 GRAMMAR: Present continuous statements

A **Write the –*ing* form of the verbs.**

1 chat _chatting_
2 do _____
3 eat _____
4 get _____
5 go _____
6 have _____
7 play _____
8 run _____
9 shop _____
10 study _____
11 take _____
12 work _____

B Complete the sentences with the present continuous form of the verbs in parentheses ( ).

1 I'm chatting _____ (chat) on the phone right now.

2 We _____ (do) the dishes in the kitchen.

3 Sara and Tomas are at a store. They _____ (shop) for new furniture.

4 Riu is in the bathroom. He _____ (take) a shower.

5 The girls are in the park. They _____ (run).

6 This game isn't boring. We _____ (have) fun.

7 The children are in bed, but they _____ (get) up now.

8 I'm in the kitchen. I _____ (eat) lunch.

## 3 GRAMMAR AND VOCABULARY

A Complete the sentences with the affirmative (+) or negative (−) form of the present continuous.

1 I usually take a shower at 7:30 a.m. It's 9:00 now.
I'm not taking _____ a shower right now.

2 Sandra doesn't cook lunch on weekdays. It's noon on Tuesday. Sandra _____ lunch at the moment.

3 Benjamin and Deb do the dishes after dinner. It's after dinner. They _____ the dishes.

4 Harry always brushes his teeth after he eats. It's after lunch. He _____ his teeth now.

5 Eva always helps her parents on the weekend. It's Saturday. She _____ her parents right now.

6 My family and I never clean our house on a weekday. It's Monday. We _____ our house.

B Circle the correct words.

1 I sometimes *take* / *am taking* a bath at night.

2 Ruiz *doesn't cook* / *isn't cooking* dinner right now.

3 The students often *do* / *are doing* their homework before class.

4 I always *am brushing* / *brush* my teeth in the morning and at night.

5 My family and I never *do* / *are doing* the dishes together.

6 Katya *cleans* / *is cleaning* her room right now.

C Look at the sentences in exercise 3B. Then write what you are doing (or not doing) right now.

1 I'm not taking a bath right now. _____

2 _____

3 _____

4 _____

5 _____

6 _____

# 7.2 TEXTING ON THE RUN

## 1 VOCABULARY: Transportation

A **Match the questions (1–6) with the answers (a–f).**

1 Are you driving to work?     _c_
2 Are you walking to work?
3 Are you at the movie theater?
4 What are you studying?
5 Are you coming home now?
6 Where are you riding your bike?

a Yes. I'm waiting for Tom.
b No. My office isn't near my house.
c Yes, I am. I drive every day.
d I'm riding it to the park.
e Yes, but I'm shopping in the mall first.
f I'm not studying right now. I'm reading.

## 2 GRAMMAR: Present continuous questions

A **Read the words and write questions.**

1 you / do / homework / right now?     _Are you doing your homework right now?_
2 your friends / play / soccer / right now?
3 your friend / send / you / a text message?
4 you and your friends / learn / English?
5 you / listen / to music / right now?

B **Answer the questions so they are true for you.**

1     Yes, I am.
2
3
4
5

C **Read the short conversations. Write the questions for B.**

1 **A** Lisa isn't waiting for her husband.

   **B** Who is she waiting for?

   **A** She's waiting for her brother.

2 **A** I'm not going to work right now.

   **B** _____

   **A** I'm going to the supermarket.

3 **A** Yoko's in the kitchen.

   **B** _____

   **A** She's studying for her exam. And drinking coffee!

4 **A** The boys are carrying some big bags.

   **B** _____

   **A** Because they're helping their aunt.

5 **A** I'm helping my daughter with her homework.

   **B** _____

   **A** Because she has an exam on Friday.

6 **A** My children are in the park.

   **B** _____

   **A** No, not soccer. They're playing basketball.

## 3 GRAMMAR AND VOCABULARY

A **You are on a train. People are talking on their cell phones. Write present continuous questions for the answers. Use the words in the box.**

| go | on the bus | ride your bike | ~~take the train~~ | wait for your friend | walk |
|---|---|---|---|---|---|

1 **A** Are you taking the train?      **B** Yes, I am. I'm visiting my friend.

2 **A** _____      **B** No, I'm not. She's here.

3 **A** _____      **B** No, I'm not. I'm on the train.

4 **A** _____      **B** I'm walking to the movie theater.

5 **A** _____      **B** I'm going to a party.

6 **A** _____      **B** No. My brother has my bike.

B **You are on a bus. People are talking on their cell phones. Write two conversations. Use the words in the box in exercise 3A.**

1 **A** _____

   **B** _____

2 **A** _____

   **B** _____

# 7.3    A NEW LIFE

## 1   FUNCTIONAL LANGUAGE: Asking how things are going

A   **Put the phone conversation in the correct order.**

| | | |
|---|---|---|
| _____ | **Jesse** | Really? Me, too. |
| 1 | **Jesse** | Hello. |
| _____ | **Jesse** | Hey, Gustavo! |
| _____ | **Jesse** | Not bad, thanks. How are you? |
| _____ | **Gustavo** | How are you doing? |
| _____ | **Gustavo** | Hi, Jesse. It's Gustavo. |
| _____ | **Gustavo** | I'm fine. I'm doing my homework right now. |

## 2   REAL-WORLD STRATEGY: Reacting to news

A   **Read the sentences. Check (✓) good news, bad news, or ordinary news. Write** *Oh, Oh wow!,* **or** *Oh no.*

| | Good news | Bad news | Ordinary news | Reaction |
|---|---|---|---|---|
| **1** I love my new job! | | | | |
| **2** I'm helping my son with his homework. | | | | |
| **3** My grandmother is 100 years old. | | | | |
| **4** There are no rooms at the hotel today. | | | | |
| **5** I have one brother and one sister. | | | | |
| **6** I'm 20 minutes late for class. | | | | |

54

## 3 FUNCTIONAL LANGUAGE AND REAL-WORLD STRATEGY

A Complete the conversation.

**Anna** ¹_____Hello._____

**Paul** Hi, Anna. ²_____ Paul.

**Anna** ³_____, Paul. How ⁴_____ you?

**Paul** Good. How are you ⁵_____?

**Anna** ⁶_____ fine, thanks. Are you at home?

**Paul** No. I'm driving to work.

**Anna** On Sunday?

**Paul** Yeah. I'm working on Sundays these days.

**Anna** Oh, ⁷_____! Why?

**Paul** I have a new job on weekends.

**Anna** ⁸_____. Do you like it?

**Paul** Yeah, I love it!

**Anna** Oh, ⁹_____! That's great.

B Read about Sylvia and Rafael. How many children does Sylvia have? What is Rafael's bad news?

Sylvia and Rafael are cousins. They live in Florida. Sylvia's children are six, nine, and fourteen years old. Sylvia is always busy – at work and at home. Rafael has some bad news. His wife, Pearl, is not in Florida right now. She is working in California.

C Sylvia and Rafael are talking. Write their conversation. Use the information in exercise 3B.

_____ _____

_____ _____

_____ _____

_____ _____

_____ _____

## 7.4 CHAOS!

## 1 READING

A  **SCAN**  Read the blog. When does the restaurant close?

### The Life of a Chef: A to Z by Chef Andy
*B is for Busy!*

[Thursday, January 15, 5:30 a.m.] I'm having breakfast at the restaurant. This is my favorite time of the day. There are no people here.

[Thursday, January 15, 6:00 a.m.] Now there are ten people in the restaurant. They're drinking coffee and chatting. The same ten people come every day from 6:00 to 7:00. Then they take the 7:10 train to work.

[Thursday, January 15, 8:30 a.m.] Here are the moms and dads with small children. They're walking to the restaurant. Now they're opening the door. Oh, no! The children are running in the restaurant. I don't like that.

[Thursday, January 15, 9:15 a.m.] I'm cooking today's lunch. The restaurant's servers, Nick and Alicia are helping me in the kitchen.

[Thursday, January 15, 11:15 a.m.] I'm eating lunch with Nick and Alicia. We always eat before people come for lunch.

[Thursday, January 15, 12:00 p.m.] It's noon now. People are waiting at the door. There are 20 people!

[Thursday, January 15, 2:30 p.m.] There usually aren't a lot of people in the restaurant in the afternoon. We're cleaning the kitchen and the tables in the dining area.

[Thursday, January 15, 4:30 p.m.] I'm cooking dinner. Mac and Pilar are helping me now. We are cooking food for 50 people! The restaurant closes at 11 p.m. It's a very busy day. But people love my food, so I love my job!

B  **READ FOR DETAILS**  Read the blog again. Then complete the chart with the times.

| | | | |
|---|---|---|---|
| 5:30 a.m. | Andy is having breakfast. | | Andy is cooking lunch. |
| | Ten people are drinking coffee and talking. | | Andy and two people are having lunch. |
| | Parents are coming to the restaurant with their children. | | People are coming for lunch at the restaurant. |
| | | | Andy is cooking dinner. |

## 2 LISTENING

A  🔊 **7.01**  **LISTEN FOR SUPPORTING DETAILS**  Listen to Andy talk about his job. Choose the correct answers.

1  How many people does Andy cook for every day?

   **a** 100          **b** four          **c** 200

2  How many days a week is the restaurant open?

   **a** seven          **b** three          **c** four

3  Why do the people like the restaurant?

   **a** because they're not cooking at home          **b** because the restaurant is busy

   **c** because they're not at work

4  What does Andy do in his free time?

   **a** cooks at home          **b** eats in restaurants          **c** helps his friends

## 3 WRITING

A **Match 1–6 with a–f. Then write sentences below. Add *too* or *also* and use the correct punctuation.**

| | | | | | |
|---|---|---|---|---|---|
| 1 | I like Nick and Alicia. | f | **a** | I cook dinner. | (too) |
| 2 | My job is busy. | | **b** | They're playing with things. | (also) |
| 3 | The children are running in the restaurant. | | **c** | I'm a writer. | (too) |
| 4 | I cook breakfast and lunch. | | **d** | They come for dinner. | (also) |
| 5 | Mr and Mrs Garcia come for breakfast on Friday. | | **e** | I work a lot of hours. | (also) |
| 6 | I'm a chef. | | **f** | I like Mac and Pilar. | (too) |

1 I like Nick and Alicia. I like Mac and Pilar, too.

2 _____

3 _____

4 _____

5 _____

6 _____

B **Add *And, But*, or *Also* to the sentences below. Use the correct punctuation.**

1 I like the blog. ___And OR Also,___ I think the comments are interesting.

2 The writer has a busy life. _____ he has fun.

3 She works in a Mexican restaurant. _____ she goes to school at night.

4 Clara and Hugo really like the Couch Café. _____ they think it's expensive.

C **Write a blog post about a day in your life. Give your blog a title (for example, *F is for Fun*). Write about what you do at different times of the day. What is your favorite time of the day? Why?**

# CHECK AND REVIEW

**Read the statements. Can you do these things?**

| UNIT 7 | Mark the boxes. ✔ I can do it. ? I am not sure. I can … | If you are not sure, go back to these pages in the Student's Book. |
|---|---|---|
| VOCABULARY | ☐ use words about activities around the house. <br> ☐ use transportation words. | page 66 <br> page 68 |
| GRAMMAR | ☐ use the present continuous in statements. <br> ☐ ask questions in the present continuous. | page 67 <br> page 69 |
| FUNCTIONAL LANGUAGE | ☐ start a phone call. <br> ☐ react to news. | page 70 <br> page 71 |
| SKILLS | ☐ write a blog about things happening now. <br> ☐ use *and, but*, and *also*. | page 73 <br> page 73 |

## 8.1 SHE LIKES MUSIC, BUT SHE CAN'T DANCE!

### 1 VOCABULARY: Verbs to describe skills

A **Look at the pictures and complete the sentences. Use the correct form of the verbs in the box.**

| dance | draw | fix things | paint | play the guitar | read music |
|-------|------|-----------|-------|-----------------|------------|
| sing | skateboard | surf | snowboard | speak two languages | ~~swim~~ |

1 Matt _____swims_____ every week.

2 Jorge is an artist and _____ beautiful pictures.

3 Sidney _____ for people.

4 Natalia is Mexican-American. She _____.

5 Renato goes to the beach every weekend and _____.

6 Ben is in a music class and _____ well.

7 Jaime _____ in the mountains in winter.

8 Aiko often goes to the park and _____.

9 Lorena _____ in a band.

10 Paola _____ with her cousin at family parties.

11 Sergei _____ his favorite music in the morning.

12 Emma _____ with her friends after school.

## 2 GRAMMAR: *can* and *can't* for ability; *well*

**A** Read the text. (Circle) *can* or *can't* to complete the sentences.

My family is from the United States. My brother and I [1](can) / *can't* speak English and Spanish. My brother lives in France now, and he [2]*can* / *can't* speak French, too. My mom only speaks English – she [3]*can* / *can't* speak other languages. My dad [4]*can* / *can't* speak other languages, but he [5]*can* / *can't* read music. He loves his piano!

We have other skills, too. My mom [6]*can* / *can't* fix things, for example the car, or our bikes. They always work well. My brother [7]*can* / *can't* draw well, and he [8]*can* / *can't* paint well, too. I love his pictures! I [9]*can* / *can't* sing well – my brother says I'm not very good. But I [10]*can* / *can't* dance – I love it!

**B** Write sentences with *can*. Use the verbs in the box and *well*.

| cook | draw | drive | play music | ~~play soccer~~ | speak English |

1  Soccer players *can play soccer* well.
2  Bus drivers _____ .
3  A chef _____ .
4  English teachers _____ .
5  An artist _____ .
6  People in a band _____ .

## 3 GRAMMAR AND VOCABULARY

**A** Complete the chart for you. Then write questions and answers with *can* or *can't* and the words in parentheses ( ).

| | dance | draw | fix things | paint | play the guitar | read music | ride a bike | sing | skateboard | snowboard | speak two languages | surf | swim |
|---|---|---|---|---|---|---|---|---|---|---|---|---|---|
| Carla | ✔ | ✗ | ✔ | ✗ | ✔ | ✔ | ✔ | ✔ | ✗ | ✗ | ✔ | ✗ | ✔ |
| Tony | ✔ | ✔ | ✔ | ✔ | ✗ | ✗ | ✔ | ✗ | ✔ | ✗ | ✔ | ✔ | ✔ |
| You | | | | | | | | | | | | | |

1  (Carla / play the guitar)          *Can Carla play the guitar? Yes, she can.*
2  (Tony / sing)
3  (Carla and Tony / snowboard)
4  (Carla and Tony / speak two languages)
5  (Carla / surf)
6  (Tony / paint)
7  (you / read music)
8  (you / fix things)

**B** Look at the answers. Write questions about people you know. Use the verbs in exercise 3A.

1  *Can your mother swim?*          Yes, she can.          4  _____  No, she can't.
2  _____          Yes, he can.          5  _____  No, they can't.
3  _____          No, he can't.          6  _____  Yes, they can.

# HAPPY WORKERS = GREAT WORKERS?

## 1 VOCABULARY: Work

A **Complete the sentences with the words in the box.**

| | | | |
|---|---|---|---|
| ~~company~~ | coworkers | have a meeting | office |
| take a break | think | work hard | workers |

I work for a big ¹____company____. Its name is Verulia. There are 250 ²_____ in my company. Some people work in the capital city, but 50 of us work in Gardon, near my home. I like my ³_____. They are very friendly. The ⁴_____ is nice because it is near a park. I usually ⁵_____ at 10:30 for half an hour. I go for a walk in the park. Sometimes 10 or 15 of us ⁶_____ in the park. It's really good because we ⁷_____ of great ideas outside. I ⁸_____ – sometimes for six days a week – but I love my job!

## 2 GRAMMAR: *can* and *can't* for possibility

A **Complete the sentences with *can* or *can't*.**

1 It's possible to swim in the lake.
   We *can swim in the lake.*_____

2 It's not possible to surf there.
   You _____

3 It's not possible to use my cell phone in the mountains.
   I _____

4 It's possible to ride our bikes in the park.
   We _____

5 Maria doesn't walk a lot. It's possible to take the bus.
   She _____

6 It's not possible for a dog to go in a restaurant.
   A dog _____

B   Write questions about your English class.
Use *can* or *can't* and the words in parentheses ( ).
Then write answers for the questions.

1   (be late for class)

   *Can you be late for class?*

   *No, I (OR we) can't.*

2   (speak your language in class)

3   (ask your teacher questions)

4   (use your cell phone in class)

5   (when / have a meeting with your teacher)

6   (what / do on your break)

## 3   GRAMMAR AND VOCABULARY

A   Look at the chart. How are New Tech Company and Best Tech Company different? Write sentences about each company. Use *can* and *can't*.

| | New Tech Company | Best Tech Company |
|---|---|---|
| work at home or in the office | ✔ | |
| work in the office every day | | ✔ |
| 30 hours a week + 10 minute coffee break every day | | ✔ |
| 50 hours a week + breaks when you want | ✔ | |
| meetings in the office three times a week | | ✔ |
| Skype meetings every month | ✔ | |

1   *At New Tech Company, you can work from home or in the office.*

2   

3   

4   

B   Do you want to work at New Tech Company or Best Tech Company? Write your answer.
Give two or three reasons.

# 8.3 ARE YOU THE RIGHT PERSON?

## 1 FUNCTIONAL LANGUAGE: Giving and asking for opinions

A **Put the words into the correct order to make questions.**

1 Do / have happy workers?/ that / you / think / great companies

   *Do you think that great companies have happy workers?*

2 Why / friends are important? / you / do / think

   _____

3 you / technology / a good thing? / is / think / Do

   _____

4 fun? / you / think / Do / school / is

   _____

5 a job? / Why / you / think / want / do / people

   _____

B **Match the questions from exercise 1A with the answers below.**

a _____ Yes. I think technology is changing the world. It's good.

b _____ I think people want a job because they want money.

c _____ Yes, I do. I think that good companies always have happy workers.

d _____ No. I think school is boring.

e _____ I think friends are important because they are fun and interesting.

C **Answer the questions so they are true for you. Give your opinion. Use** *I think so* **or** *I don't think so.*

1 Are you good at sports?        *I don't think so.*

2 Are you a good worker?        _____

3 Are you good at video games?   _____

4 Are you a good coworker?       _____

5 Are you good at teamwork?      _____

## 2 REAL-WORLD STRATEGY: Explaining and saying more about an idea

A **Circle *a* or *b* to complete the sentences.**

1 I think this is a great company. I mean,

   (a) It's a good place to work.

   b I'm a really good worker.

2 We love our dog. I mean,

   a her name is Kiki.

   b she's always fun and happy.

3 My coworkers are great. I mean,

   a we work well together.

   b we work in the same office.

4 I'm not very good at soccer. I mean,

   a I watch soccer on TV, but I can't *play* soccer.

   b I watch soccer with my friends a lot.

A  **Bill has an interview for a job at a restaurant. Use the expressions in the box to complete the conversation.**

> Do you think that …    I don't think so.    I mean, …    I think so.

**Chef**  Are you the right person for this job?

**Bill**  Yeah. [1]_____

**Chef**  Why are you a good server?

**Bill**  Because on weekends, I go to different restaurants with my friends, and I see a lot of servers. The good servers are friendly. I'm friendly, too.

**Chef**  OK. [2]_____ it's important to work well with other servers?

**Bill**  [3]_____ . I mean, servers don't work with other servers.

**Chef**  Really? In my restaurant, teamwork is important. The servers work with the chefs in the kitchen.

**Bill**  Oh.

**Chef**  Our busy days are Friday, Saturday, and Sunday. Can you work then?

**Bill**  I can't work on Saturday and Sunday. [4]_____ I'm busy on weekends. But I can work on Tuesday, Wednesday, and Thursday.

B  **Is Bill is the right person for the job? Why or why not?**

_____

_____

C  **Write a conversation between the chef and a woman, Sofia. The chef thinks Sofia is the right person for the job.**

_____

_____

_____

_____

_____

_____

_____

_____

_____

_____

_____

_____

# 8.4 COMPUTERS AND OUR JOBS

## 1 LISTENING

A 🔊 **8.01** **LISTEN FOR DETAILS** Listen to part of a podcast about robots. What do Emily and Joel think? ⃝Circle the correct answer.

Emily and Joel *think / do not think* that a robot can be a child's friend.

B 🔊 **8.01** **LISTEN FOR SUPPORTING DETAILS** Listen again. What is good about robots for children? Check (✓) the things Emily and Joel say.

1 Children can play games with robots. ☐
2 Children can learn about technology from robots. ☐
3 Children can play soccer with robots. ☐
4 Robots and children can have birthday parties. ☐
5 Robots are not real friends. ☐
6 Children can do things with robots all day. ☐

## 2 READING

A Read the article. Then choose the correct title. ⃝Circle 1, 2, or 3.

1 New Robots
2 Our Grandparents' Problems
3 Robots for Our Grandparents

> Companies now have talking robots for grandparents. Sometimes, our grandparents do not live with other people. They do not talk to other people every day and they don't see their friends often. This is a problem, and the new robots can help.
>
> Elena Cho is an example. She is an old woman. She doesn't live with her family. But now, she has a talking robot. It can tell her about new books or interesting movies. Also, it can play music for Elena. Her robot knows her favorite songs and singers.
>
> Elena Cho says, "My robot is not a friend, but I like it very much."

B Read the article again. Check (✓) the correct sentences.

1 Some grandparents do not live with other people. ✔
2 New robots can help grandparents. ____
3 Elena Cho's robot goes to the movies with her. ____
4 Elena Cho's robot plays her favorite music. ____
5 Elena doesn't like her robot. ____

## 3 WRITING

A  **Read three people's online comments about the podcast. Find the quotes from Emily and Joel. Change the punctuation for the quotes.**

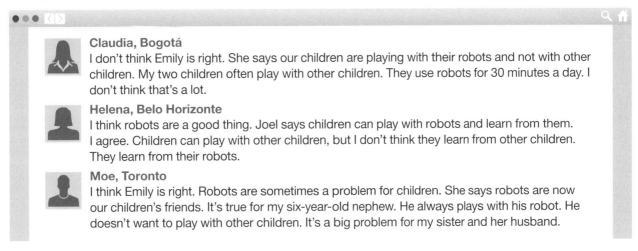

**Claudia, Bogotá**
I don't think Emily is right. She says our children are playing with their robots and not with other children. My two children often play with other children. They use robots for 30 minutes a day. I don't think that's a lot.

**Helena, Belo Horizonte**
I think robots are a good thing. Joel says children can play with robots and learn from them. I agree. Children can play with other children, but I don't think they learn from other children. They learn from their robots.

**Moe, Toronto**
I think Emily is right. Robots are sometimes a problem for children. She says robots are now our children's friends. It's true for my six-year-old nephew. He always plays with his robot. He doesn't want to play with other children. It's a big problem for my sister and her husband.

B  **Look at the sentences about robots for old people. Change the sentences to quotes. Use *says* or *said* and the correct punctuation.**

**Informal writing:**

1  Elena Cho: I like my new talking robot.

2  Elena Cho's son: The robot helps my mother a lot.

**Formal writing:**

3  Ronaldo Benson: Our company makes robots for grandparents.

4  Doctor Wu: Robots are good for grandparents because their families don't see them every day.

C  **Write an online comment. Give your opinion about robots for grandparents.**

# CHECK AND REVIEW

**Read the statements. Can you do these things?**

| UNIT 8 | Mark the boxes.  ✔ I can do it.   ? I am not sure.<br>I can … | If you are not sure, go back to these pages in the Student's Book. |
|---|---|---|
| VOCABULARY | ☐ use verbs to describe skills. | page 76 |
|  | ☐ use words about work. | page 78 |
| GRAMMAR | ☐ use *can* or *can't* for ability. | page 77 |
|  | ☐ use *well*. | page 77 |
|  | ☐ use *can* or *can't* for possibility. | page 79 |
| FUNCTIONAL LANGUAGE | ☐ ask for and give opinions. | page 80 |
|  | ☐ explain and say more about an idea. | page 81 |
| SKILLS | ☐ write an online comment. | page 83 |
|  | ☐ use quotations for other people's words. | page 83 |

### 1    VOCABULARY: Travel

A    **Complete the sentences with the words in the box.**

| | | | |
|---|---|---|---|
| boat | country | plane | ranch |
| tickets | tour | town | ~~vacation~~ |

1    Silvia and Raúl aren't working. They are on _____vacation_____ .

2    Raúl loves animals. He's on a farm in the _____, away from the city.

3    Silvia loves the ocean. She goes on a _____ on the water.

4    Silvia and Raúl buy _____ for the museum. They are $25 each.

5    Silvia doesn't like animals. A _____ is not a good place for her.

6    Silvia lives in a small _____. It has 10,000 people.

7    Silvia and Raúl go on a _____ of the museum. A woman tells them about the interesting art.

8    Silvia sits next to Raúl on the _____. She looks out the window and sees buildings and trees.

### 2    GRAMMAR: *This* and *These*

A    **Complete the conversations. Use *this* or *these* and the words in the box.**

| | | |
|---|---|---|
| museum | photos | seats |
| your hotel | your tickets | ~~your train~~ |

1    **A**  Is _____this your train_____ ?

    **B**  Yes, it is. We're going home.

2    **A**  Are _____ ?

    **B**  Yes. We need them for the movie.

3    **A**  _____ cool.

    **B**  Yes. They are from our vacation.

4    **A**  Is _____ ?

    **B**  Yes, our room is very nice!

5    **A**  Wow, _____ comfortable.

    **B**  Yes, they are.

6    **A**  _____ interesting.

    **B**  Yes. It has a lot of beautiful pictures.

A   Look at the pictures from people's vacations. Imagine you are writing messages about each trip. Write
    two or three sentences for each picture. Use *this* or *these*. How many words from the box can you use?

boat     country     farm     ranch     plane     ticket     tour     town     vacation

1   We're on a bike tour. There are many interesting
    places on the tour. It's not boring!

2   _____

3   _____

# SAN FRANCISCO, HERE WE COME

## 1 VOCABULARY: Travel arrangements

A Cross out the words that do **not** complete the sentences.

| | | | | |
|---|---|---|---|---|
| 1 | We have to arrive _____ at 2 p.m. | at our destination | at the airport | ~~on a trip~~ |
| 2 | They are buying _____ . | friends | some coffee | tickets |
| 3 | The flight _____ at 10 a.m. | arrives | leaves | stays |
| 4 | We are _____ my aunt's house. | checking in at | staying at | traveling to |
| 5 | Our _____ is from June 15 to July 1. | destination | trip | vacation |
| 6 | We can check in at the _____ . | airport | hotel | museum |
| 7 | We _____ on the plane for 12 hours. | arrive | fly | travel |
| 8 | People can buy plane tickets _____ . | at the airport | online | on a flight |

## 2 GRAMMAR: *like to, want to, need to, have to*

A Circle the correct answers.

1 My husband has a business trip this week. He *has to* / *likes to* go to Boston.

2 This is our favorite restaurant. We *like to* / *need to* go there for lunch on Sunday.

3 My brother is studying to be a doctor. He *wants to* / *needs to* study for five years.

4 This camera is not in the stores. You *want to* / *have to* buy it online.

5 Can we take the bus to the mall? I don't *have to* / *want to* drive.

6 My friends and I are learning Chinese. *We want to* / *need to* go to China on vacation next year.

7 I *like to* / *have to* eat cookies for breakfast, but I know it's bad for me.

8 My friend *wants to* / *likes to* work at a big technology company. She has an interview there next week!

B   **Complete the sentences with affirmative (+) or negative (–) forms of *have to*, *like to*, *need to*, or *want to*. Sometimes there are two correct answers.**

1   It's 10 a.m. My flight is at 12 p.m. I'm late! I ___need to OR have to___ go to the airport.

2   My sister _____ go on vacation with our parents. She likes to travel with her friends.

3   Jason's very hungry. He _____ eat dinner now.

4   Sari _____ travel on the subway. It's busy and hot.

5   My parents' car is very old. They _____ buy a new car.

6   We're planning our next vacation. We _____ go to a lot of interesting places.

## 3 GRAMMAR AND VOCABULARY

A   **Write sentences that are true for you.**

1   have / check in / three hours before my flight

   *I have to check in three hours before my flight at the airport near my city.*

2   like / fly

   _____

3   have / buy plane tickets online

   _____

4   like / stay at hotels

   _____

5   need / arrive / at the bus stop 15 minutes early

   _____

6   want / work / at an airport

   _____

7   need / leave / home before 8:00 a.m.

   _____

8   like / take / trips to places near my home

   _____

9   want / travel / to New York

   _____

## 1 FUNCTIONAL LANGUAGE: Asking for missing information and clarification

A **Correct four mistakes in the conversations.**

   **1** **A** Excuse me. Where ~~the~~ is the women's restroom?

      **B** It's over there, near the door.

   **2** **A** Excuse me. What time the bus to San Diego leave?

      **B** It leaves at 11:15 a.m.

   **3** **A** Excuse me. How much this guide book?

      **B** It's $12.99.

   **4** **A** Excuse me. I need buy a ticket to Bogotá. How much is it?

      **B** A bus ticket $147.

B **Put the conversation in the correct order.**

| | | |
|---|---|---|
| ____ | **A** | And for a child? Is it the same price? |
| 1 | **A** | Excuse me. How much is one ticket? |
| ____ | **A** | Then one ticket for me and one ticket for my son, please. |
| ____ | **A** | Where are seats 10A and 10B? |
| ____ | **B** | Tickets are $15. |
| 8 | **B** | They're on the right. |
| ____ | **B** | OK. Your seats are 10A and 10B. |
| ____ | **B** | No, it isn't. Tickets for children are $5. |

## 2 REAL-WORLD STRATEGY: Asking someone to repeat something

A **Check (✓) two correct ways to ask someone to repeat something.**

   **1** Sorry, repeat, please.   ____

   **2** Sorry, can you repeat that, please?   ____

   **3** Sorry, what you say?   ____

   **4** Sorry, can you say that again?   ____

## 3 FUNCTIONAL LANGUAGE AND REAL-WORLD STRATEGY

A   **Mia is at a store. She talks to a clerk. Use the information below to write their conversation.**

1   Mia wants to know the price of the flowers.
2   The clerk says a price.
3   Mia wants to know the price of a plant, too.
4   The clerk says a price for the flowers and the plant together.
5   Mia doesn't understand.
6   The clerk repeats the information.

7   Mia understands. Now she wants to know where a good café is.
8   The clerk gives directions.
9   Mia doesn't understand.
10  The clerk repeats the directions.
11  Mia thanks the clerk.
12  The clerk finishes the conversation.

1   **Mia**   Excuse me. How much are the flowers?
2   **Clerk**
3   **Mia**
4   **Clerk**
5   **Mia**
6   **Clerk**
7   **Mia**
8   **Clerk**
9   **Mia**
10  **Clerk**
11  **Mia**
12  **Clerk**

# A GREAT DESTINATION

## 1 READING

A **SKIM** **Skim the article. Check (✓) the things the article mentions.**

☐ horses        ☐ museums      ☐ hotels

☐ countries in South America      ☐ food

**GLOSSARY**
**ride a horse** (*v*) sit on a horse

### South American ranch vacations

**Do you like animals and nature? Do you want to travel and meet people? Why not visit a *gaucho* ranch?**

A *gaucho* ranch is a very big farm with horses and other animals. The workers there are called *gauchos*. They are really good with horses. People can visit *gaucho* ranches and learn about the farm and the animals.

Can you ride a horse well? The *gauchos* can take you on a tour of the ranch.

Do you want to learn to ride a horse? The *gauchos* can help you!

There are *gaucho* ranches in South America, for example in Argentina, Bolivia, Chile, and Uruguay. You can visit for a week, or you can work on a *gaucho* ranch for a month. Some ranches even have one-day tours.

You don't have to ride a horse every day. You can also walk around the ranch and see all the interesting plants and animals.

Maybe you don't want to go to the country, but you're interested in ranches. Some towns near ranches have *gaucho* museums. One *gaucho* museum is only 90 minutes from Buenos Aires. You can go there and learn a lot about *gaucho* life. Also, the museum is free!

So, go to a *gaucho* ranch and have a great vacation!

An Argentinian *gaucho* on his horse

B **Read the article again. Answer the questions. Write complete sentences.**

1 Where does a gaucho work?

2 What countries have gaucho ranches?

3 How long can you stay at a gaucho ranch?

4 What can you learn about in a gaucho museum?

## 2 LISTENING

A 🔊 **9.01** **LISTEN FOR DETAILS** **Listen to Ella talk about her vacation. Does she like it?**

B 🔊 **9.01** **LISTEN FOR SUPPORTING DETAILS** **Listen again. Choose the correct answer.**

1 Ella is visiting _____.

   **a** a ranch        **b** an island      **c** a museum

2 What does Ella think about the people there?

   **a** They are interesting.    **b** They are different.    **c** They are friendly.

3 What can Ella do in the afternoon?

   **a** cook lunch        **b** go for a walk      **c** talk to her mother

4 Next year, Ella wants to _____.

   **a** come with her mother    **b** stay longer      **c** get a bigger room

## 3 WRITING

A  Read the advice below. Complete the paragraphs with affirmative (+) and negative (–) imperative verbs in the box.

drive    eat    go x2    ~~read~~    ride    take

**How to plan your ranch vacation**

Ranch vacations in Argentina are great, but ¹_____read_____ the online reviews before you go. ²_____ from October to December or from April to June. These are good times to visit. ³_____ from January to March. It can be very hot. Some ranches are hundreds of miles from Buenos Aires. ⁴_____ to the ranches in a car. It's very far. ⁵_____ a plane and then a taxi.

Is this your first time on a horse? You can have lessons on the ranch. They're not expensive. Or can you ride a horse well? ⁶_____ to a different part of the ranch every day. Ranches are really big. You need to visit for a week or two!

⁷_____ a lot at lunch. Dinner is a big meal, and the food is great!

B  Change the formal sentences to informal sentences. Use imperatives.

1  You need to come for a week.          *Come for a week.*

2  You can visit the place in August.    _____

3  You have to take a taxi.              _____

4  You need to eat a big breakfast       _____

C  Think about a place you like. Write about what people can do and see there. Use imperatives to give advice.

# CHECK AND REVIEW

**Read the statements. Can you do these things?**

| UNIT 9 | Mark the boxes. ☑ I can do it.  ? I am not sure.<br>I can … | If you are not sure, go back to these pages in the Student's Book. |
|---|---|---|
| VOCABULARY | ☐ use travel words.<br>☐ use words for travel arrangements. | page 86<br>page 88 |
| GRAMMAR | ☐ use *this* and *these*.<br>☐ use *like to, want to, have to,* and *need to*. | page 87<br>page 89 |
| FUNCTIONAL LANGUAGE | ☐ ask for and give missing information.<br>☐ ask someone to repeat something. | page 90<br>page 91 |
| SKILLS | ☐ write a description of a place.<br>☐ use imperatives to give advice. | page 93<br>page 93 |

# 10.1 WHITE NIGHTS

## 1 VOCABULARY: Going out

A **Use the words in the box to complete the conversation.**

| eat | get | go | have | look at | meet | take x2 |

**A** What do you usually do on the weekend? I need ideas!

**B** I visit the mall and ¹_____ shopping. Sometimes I ²_____ together with friends. What about you?

**A** I like to go to the museum near my home and ³_____ art. I like to ⁴_____ a walk outside, too. I often go to the park.

**B** The park is great! You can ⁵_____ a picnic in the park. It's fun to ⁶_____ outside!

**A** Good idea! I never have picnics in the park. Usually I ⁷_____ my husband out to dinner at our favorite restaurant. But not this weekend.

**B** Oh? Why not? Where is he?

**A** He's in New York right now. He's going to be home next week. I want to ⁸_____ him at the airport.

## 2 GRAMMAR: Statements with *be going to*

A **Imagine that it is 10 a.m. on Thursday, July 6. Look at the future plans below. Replace the <u>underlined</u> words with future time expressions from the box. You won't use all the words.**

| next month | on Saturday | this weekend | next Saturday | this afternoon |
| this year | next week | this month | tomorrow | next weekend |
| this Saturday | tonight | next year | this week | |

1 I'm going to swim <u>in six hours</u>.

   I'm going to swim this afternoon.

2 The doctor is going to call <u>in 24 hours</u>.

   _____

3 Miriam is going to have a party <u>on August 6</u>.

   _____

4 We're going to meet our friend <u>in two days</u>.

   _____

5 We're going to buy the tickets <u>in 10 hours</u>.

   _____

6 They aren't going to have a picnic <u>in seven days</u>.

   _____

B  **Write sentences with *be going to*.**

1  It's Monday today. I meet my friends every Tuesday.

   I'm going to meet my friends tomorrow _____.

2  Felipe takes a walk every night.

   _____ tonight.

3  Marco and his friends go to the mall every weekend.

   _____ next weekend.

4  Sara doesn't want to take a trip next year.

   _____ next year.

5  Kate and her coworkers take a break every day at 11:00.

   _____ this morning at 11:00.

6  I have class every Tuesday.

   _____ on Tuesday.

**3**  **GRAMMAR AND VOCABULARY**

A  **Look at Simon's plans for Friday, Saturday, and Sunday. Write sentences about what he is going to do.**

| Thursday | Friday | Saturday | Sunday |
|----------|--------|----------|--------|
| Today! | Meet my friend at the airport | Picnic at the beach | Go shopping at the mall |
|  | Take my friend out for dinner |  | Free time |

1  On Friday, Simon is going to meet his friend at the airport.

2  _____

3  _____

4  _____

5  _____

B  **Write five true sentences about you. Use the words in exercise 1A, *be going to*, and future time expressions from exercise 2A.**

1  I'm going to meet my sister tomorrow afternoon. Then we're going to go shopping.

2  _____

3  _____

4  _____

5  _____

6  _____

# BUT IT'S SUMMER THERE!

## 1 VOCABULARY: Clothes; seasons

A **Cross out the word that does <u>not</u> belong in each sentence.**

1 jeans     pants     ~~T-shirt~~        4 shorts     sweater     skirt

2 shorts     coat     hat            5 sweater     shirt     boots

3 dress     shoes     boots        6 pants     skirt     jeans

B **Read the descriptions of clothes. Which season is each person talking about? Write words in the box.**

| dry season | fall | rainy season | spring | summer | winter |
|---|---|---|---|---|---|

1 There's no rain, and it's hot! I wear shorts every day.    _dry season_

2 It's very cold! I'm wearing a coat and a hat. _____

3 I'm on the beach. I'm wearing shorts and a T-shirt, and no shoes! _____

4 It's not summer, but I can see new flowers. I'm wearing a shirt and pants.
I don't need to wear a sweater. _____

5 There's a lot of rain, but it's not cold. I'm wearing a coat and my big boots. _____

6 I'm wearing a dress. I have a coat, but I'm not wearing it. The next season is winter. _____

## 2 GRAMMAR: Questions with *be going to*

A **Read the sentences and complete the questions. Then answer the questions so they are true for you. Write short answers.**

1 I'm not going to get together with friends this weekend.

   _Are you going to get together_ _____ with friends next weekend?

   _____ _Yes, I am. OR No, I'm not._ _____

2 My friend isn't going to meet me tonight.

   _____ you tomorrow?

   _____

3 My family and I aren't going to be on vacation this month.

   _____ next month?

   _____

4 My friends aren't going to take me out to dinner this week.

   _____ you out to dinner next week?

   _____

5 My teacher isn't going to work this summer.

   _____ next summer?

   _____

6 I'm not going to buy a car in the spring.

   _____ next fall?

B **Write questions for the answers. Use *What*, *When*, *Where*, or *Who*.**

1  A  *Who are you going to meet?*
   B  I'm going to meet my cousins.

2  A  _____
   B  The class is going to take a break in 20 minutes.

3  A  _____
   B  The stores are going to open at 9 a.m.

4  A  _____
   B  We're going to go shopping at the mall.

5  A  _____
   B  My brother is going to buy a TV.

6  A  _____
   B  I'm going to visit my parents.

## 3 GRAMMAR AND VOCABULARY

A  **Use the words to write questions. Then write true answers. Use *be going to*.**

1  who / you / visit / this fall
   *Who are you going to visit this fall?*
   *I'm going to visit my friend in Canada.*

2  who / go / with / you / on your trip


3  what clothes / you / take / on your next trip


4  when / you / buy / boots


5  what / country / you / travel / in the rainy season?


6  where / your friend / wear / her new dress


7  where / your cousin / buy / new pants


8  when / you / wear / a sweater

# 10.3 LET'S MEET AT THE HOTEL

## 1 FUNCTIONAL LANGUAGE: Making and responding to suggestions

**A Look at the conversations. Circle the correct responses.**

1  **A** There's a good Chinese restaurant near here.
   **B** a  Why don't we eat Chinese food?
      (b) Why don't we walk there?

2  **A** I don't want to cook dinner tonight.
   **B** a  Let's eat at home.
      b  Let's go to a restaurant.

3  **A** It's a beautiful day outside.
   **B** a  Why don't we take a walk?
      b  Why don't we watch a movie?

4  **A** The museum is 15 kilometers from here.
   **B** a  Let's walk to the museum.
      b  Let's take a bus.

5  **A** Let's eat outside.
   **B** a  Yes, we do.
      b  Good idea.

6  **A** Why don't we have a picnic on Sunday?
   **B** a  Sorry, I'm busy.
      b  No, we don't.

7  **A** Why don't we meet at the hotel?
   **B** a  Yes, sure.
      b  Let's meet at the hotel.

8  **A** Let's go to the beach.
   **B** a  I'm sorry.
      b  OK, sounds good.

## 2 REAL-WORLD STRATEGY: Saying why you can't do something

**A Look at Amy's week below. Then write her responses to sentences 1–5. Use _have to_.**

> *Things to do next week:*
>
> **Monday — Friday** — work from 8 a.m.–4 p.m.
>
> **Monday** — doctor, 6 p.m.
>
> **Tuesday** — make dinner for my family
>
> **Saturday** — Aunt Beatriz's party
>
> **Sunday** — study

1  Let's go to the mall Monday evening.      **Amy**  I'm sorry, but I can't. I have to go to the doctor.
2  Why don't we meet for lunch on Friday?      **Amy**  _____
3  Let's have dinner together on Tuesday.      **Amy**  _____
4  Why don't we get together on Saturday?      **Amy**  _____
5  Let's go to the beach on Sunday.      **Amy**  _____

## 3 FUNCTIONAL LANGUAGE AND REAL-WORLD STRATEGY

A   **Alex and Jay are making plans for their friend Keiko's birthday. Put the sentences in the correct order.**

| | | |
|---|---|---|
| _____ | **Keiko** | Hello. |
| _____ | **Alex** | Good idea. Let's go to the new Korean restaurant on First Street. It's really good. |
| 1 | **Alex** | So, it's Keiko's birthday on Friday. |
| _____ | **Keiko** | I'm sorry, but I can't. I'm busy then. My family is going to have a birthday party for me. Hey, why don't you and Alex come to the party? |
| _____ | **Alex** | Hi, Keiko. It's Alex. Jay and I are talking about your birthday. We want to take you out for dinner. Why don't we meet at the new Korean restaurant next Friday? |
| _____ | **Jay** | OK, great. Let's call Keiko and ask her. |
| _____ | **Jay** | Oh, yeah! Why don't we take her out to dinner for her birthday? |
| 9 | **Alex** | Thanks, Keiko. We love birthday parties. We can take you out to dinner next weekend. |
| _____ | **Alex** | Sure. I have her number on my phone. I'm calling her now … |

B   **Read the information below. Then write a conversation.**

You are making plans with two friends for next weekend. Talk about what you are going to do and when you are going to do it. You and your friends are not free at the same time. Find a time to get together.

_____

_____

_____

_____

_____

_____

_____

# 10.4 A 24-HOUR CITY

## 1 LISTENING

A 🔊 **10.01** **LISTEN FOR DETAILS** Listen to Susana talk about her trip to Stockholm, Sweden. Check (✓) the things Susana says about Stockholm.

☐ It's famous.

☐ There are old buildings.

☐ There are a lot of things to do.

☐ It's not hot.

B 🔊 **10.01** **LISTEN FOR SUPPORTING DETAILS** Listen again. Put the things to do in the order Susana says them. Cross out the sentences that she does not talk about.

_____ **a** go to a museum

_____ **b** go to the beach

_____ **c** go to an island

_____ **d** find a place to go dancing

_____ **e** go shopping and eat something

_____ **f** go for a bike ride

__1__ **g** tour famous places

_____ **h** have a picnic

## 2 READING

A Read the article about Midsummer Day in Sweden. Write *T* if the sentence is true or *F* if the sentence is false.

*Midsummer Day* is a very important day in Sweden. There is sun in the day *and* night. The holiday is on June 24, but the activities are always on the weekend. People wear holiday clothes for the day's activities, and they wear flowers, too. Children and adults dance and play games. They eat different foods – and the first strawberries of summer. Midsummer is also a time of love. Girls and young women take home seven different flowers. When they go to sleep on Midsummer Night, they see who their husband is going to be. Midsummer Day is really an important day.

strawberries

Midsummer Day in Sweden

__T__ **1** It is always in June.

_____ **2** Midsummer Day is only for children.

_____ **3** People wear different clothes.

_____ **4** Flowers are important.

## 3 WRITING

A  Read the online invitation. <u>Underline</u> <u>six</u> full forms. Change the full forms to contractions.

**Event**   Beach party!
**Host**    Brianna
**When?**   Saturday, June 20
**Where?**  Miami Beach

### Message from Brianna

Jeff's
<u>Jeff is</u> going to be 25 on June 10. We are going to have a
beach party for him. Be at Miami Beach near Fifth Street
at 6:00 p.m. We are going to have a big picnic. Then we
are going to go out. It is going to be a fun night! Do not
tell Jeff about the party. He does not know about it.

B  (Circle) the contractions in the sentences. Write *F* if the sentence is formal. Write *I* if the sentence is informal.

1  There's going to be dancing.                          I
2  Jenny is going to send the invitation.           _____
3  I am going to ask 30 people to come to the party.  _____
4  We're going to have a lot of fun.                 _____
5  Do not be late.                                   _____

C  Imagine it's a friend's birthday party. Write an invitation for their party. Describe what you are going to do. Use contractions.

# CHECK AND REVIEW

**Read the statements. Can you do these things?**

| UNIT 10 | Mark the boxes.  ✔ I can do it.  ? I am not sure. | If you are not sure, go back to these pages in the Student's Book. |
|---|---|---|
| | I can … | |
| VOCABULARY | ☐ use words for going out activities.<br>☐ use words for clothes and seasons. | page 98<br>page 100 |
| GRAMMAR | ☐ use *be going to* in statements.<br>☐ use *be going to* in *yes/no* and information questions. | page 99<br>page 101 |
| FUNCTIONAL LANGUAGE | ☐ make and respond to suggestions.<br>☐ say why I can't do something. | page 102<br>page 103 |
| SKILLS | ☐ write an online invitation.<br>☐ use contractions. | page 105<br>page 105 |

## 11.1 FLASHBACK FRIDAY

### 1 VOCABULARY: Describing people, places, and things

A Match the adjectives (1–5) with their opposites (a–e).

1 awful _____e_____          a boring
2 exciting _____        b noisy
3 fast _____            c old
4 new _____             d slow
5 quiet _____           e wonderful

B Cross out the word that people do __not__ use with *beautiful* and *cute*.

1 **beautiful**   day   girl   man   picture   woman
2 **cute**        class   dog   dress   little boy   little girl

### 2 GRAMMAR: Statements with *was* and *were*

A Complete the sentences with *was*, *wasn't*, *were*, or *weren't*.

1 I'm tall now, but I _____wasn't_____ a tall child.

2 My grandparents are always home now, but in 2015, they _____ at work.

3 We're in the same class now, but we _____ in the same class last year.

4 Gabriel is in college now, but in 2016, he _____ in high school.

5 I'm not on vacation now, but I _____ on vacation last week.

6 School is fun now, but it _____ fun before.

7 Yessica is good at basketball now, but she _____ good last year.

8 You're here now, but you _____ here at 10 o'clock.

9 My friends are in college now, but they _____ last year.

10 Sergio _____ at our company last year, but now he is.

11 It _____ nice and quiet in my house this morning because my children _____ asleep.

12 I _____ in the office all week, but I'm not today because it's Sunday!

B   Read the postcard. Then complete the sentences with *was*, *wasn't*, *were*, or *weren't*.

July 10
Hi Leonor,
Tony and I are having a wonderful vacation.
We're at the beach right now. He's swimming,
and I'm writing this postcard! This beach is
beautiful, but it's noisy. There are a lot of
really cute children here, and they're playing
near us. But that's OK. It's a beautiful day,
and we're having a great time.
How are you?
Love,
Ines

1   It's August now. Ines _____ on vacation in July.
2   Ines's parents _____ with her.
3   Ines and Tony _____ at the beach on July 10.
4   The beach _____ quiet.
5   There _____ a lot of children.

## 3   GRAMMAR AND VOCABULARY

A   Read the sentences. Then write two sentences that are the opposite. Use *wasn't* or *weren't* for A.
Use *was* or *were* for B.

1   I was quiet in class.
    A   I wasn't quiet in class. _____        B   I was noisy in class. _____

2   I was awful at sports in school.
    A   _____        B   _____

3   My school was in an old neighborhood.
    A   _____        B   _____

4   New books were boring for me.
    A   _____        B   _____

5   My first job was wonderful.
    A   _____        B   _____

6   My friends and I were noisy.
    A   _____        B   _____

7   My first computer was new.
    A   _____        B   _____

8   I was a good student.
    A   _____        B   _____

# 11.2 OUR OLD PHONE WAS GREEN

## 1 VOCABULARY: Colors

**A** Unscramble the color words.

1 ckbal _____
2 earong _____
3 twihe _____
4 dre _____
5 llowye _____
6 gary _____
7 lbeu _____
8 pkni _____
9 neerg _____
10 nrowb _____
11 lepurp _____

**B** Complete the sentences so they are true for you. Use color words from exercise 1A.

1 My cell phone is _____.
2 My favorite shirt is _____.
3 My bag is _____.
4 I'm wearing _____ clothes today.
5 I don't like the color _____.

## 2 GRAMMAR: Questions with *was* and *were*

**A** Complete the *yes/no* questions with *was* or *were*. Then answer the questions so they are true for you. Use short answers.

1 I wasn't at home on Sunday.

  <u>Were you at home on Saturday?</u> _____     <u>Yes, I was. OR No, I wasn't.</u>

2 My family and I weren't on vacation in August.

  _____ on vacation in June? _____

3 I wasn't in class on Tuesday.

  _____ in class on Wednesday? _____

4 My cousins weren't in college in 2016.

  _____ in college in 2017? _____

5 My friends weren't busy on Saturday.

  _____ busy on Friday? _____

6 My teacher wasn't at work on Sunday.

  _____ at work on Monday? _____

B   **Use the words to write questions with *was* or *were*. Then answer the questions so they are true for you.**

1   what / your first teacher's name

    What was your first teacher's name?                      My first teacher's name was Ms. Song.

2   where / your first school

3   how old / you / in 2005

4   what color / your first cell phone

5   where / you / on Saturday night

6   who / with you / on the weekend


**GRAMMAR AND VOCABULARY**

A   **Read the questions about when you were a child. Correct the mistake in each question. Then answer the questions so they are true for you.**

1   What things was brown in your home?
                  *were*

    Our kitchen table and chairs were brown.

2   What your favorite color was?

3   What color were your favorite toy?

4   Was your shoes always black?

5   Your desk was white?

6   Are there gray walls in your first home?

# I HAVE NO IDEA

## 1 FUNCTIONAL LANGUAGE: Expressing uncertainty

A Erica and Chris are at a party. Erica asks questions about the people she sees. Circle the correct words to complete the conversation.

**Erica** Who's that man over there?

**Chris** [1]I'm *not / no* sure. [2]I *think / know* he's Alma's brother.

**Erica** OK. And who's the woman next to him?

**Chris** Oh, that's Jamie's wife. Her name is Mischa, [3]I *know / think*.

**Erica** Right. Where's Alma? It's her birthday party and I can't see her!

**Chris** [4]I have *no / not* idea!

**Erica** There's Jamie. [5]*Maybe / Yeah* Jamie can tell us!

## 2 REAL-WORLD STRATEGY: Taking time to think

A Chris needs time to think about Erica's questions. Write *Let me think*, *Uh*, or *Um* in the conversation. There can sometimes be more than one answer.

**Erica** Do you need more food, Chris?

**Chris** _____, I'm not hungry, thanks.

**Erica** What time do you want to leave?

**Chris** _____. Maybe in an hour?

**Erica** Do you want to dance?

**Chris** _____, yeah!

FUNCTIONAL LANGUAGE AND REAL-WORLD STRATEGY

A  **Read sentences 1–5. Write a conversation between you and a friend. Use the words in the box in your friend's answers.**

| | | | |
|---|---|---|---|
| I have no idea. | Uh, … | I don't know. | I think … |
| Maybe … | Um, … | Let me think. | I'm not sure. |

1  You want to know Leonardo DiCaprio's age in *Titanic*.

    **You**    How old was Leonardo DiCaprio in *Titanic*?

    **Your friend**    Uh, I don't know.

2  You want to know where Leonardo DiCaprio's parents are from.

    **You**

    **Your friend**

3  You want to know the name of the actor in a TV show.

    **You**

    **Your friend**

4  You want to know when a movie was popular.

    **You**

    **Your friend**

5  You want to know who is in a famous band.

    **You**

    **Your friend**

# THINGS WE KEEP

## 1 READING

A   **SKIM**   Read the article. Find <u>three</u> reasons why people keep things.

### Why do we keep things?

Old toys. Old music. Old soccer balls. Why are they so important? Why do we keep them? Here are three reasons:

#### Our feelings

5 Maybe your favorite toy when you were a child was from your grandparents. You don't play with the toy now. You never see it. But you still want to keep it. Why? Because it's from your grandparents. You love them very much. So you
10 keep the toy.

#### Money

Do you have your parents' old music? Maybe the music was five dollars in the 1970s. Maybe it is going to be 50 or 100 dollars in 20 years. Sometimes we keep things because we can get money for them in the future.

15 #### The future

Why are you keeping your old soccer ball or your old guitar? You don't need them now. You don't play soccer or the guitar. But maybe your son or daughter is going to be a great soccer player or a wonderful guitar player. You're keeping them for your children.

B   **READ FOR DETAIL**   Read words 1–5 below. Circle the words in the article. Then match the words with their meanings (a–g). You don't need to use all the meanings.

| | | | | | | |
|---|---|---|---|---|---|---|
| **1** | it (*line 7*) | _g_ | **a** | children | **f** | things |
| **2** | them (*line 9*) | ____ | **b** | grandparents | **g** | toy |
| **3** | it (*line 13*) | ____ | **c** | music | | |
| **4** | them (*line 14*) | ____ | **d** | parents | | |
| **5** | them (*line 18*) | ____ | **e** | soccer ball or guitar | | |

## 2 LISTENING

A   🔊 **11.01**   **LISTEN FOR DETAILS**   Listen to the conversation. Write *T* for True and *F* for False.

     **1** Tadeo and Jen are shopping for old things.

     **2** School wasn't very important for Tadeo.

     **3** Tadeo's teacher was good.

B   🔊 **11.01**   **LISTEN FOR SUPPORTING DETAILS**   Listen to the conversation again. What does Tadeo keep? Does he keep it because it's expensive, or because he loves it?

## 3 WRITING

A  Read Ichiko's email. Write the correct topic sentences (a–c) for the paragraphs (1–3).

> a  There's a photo of you and me at the airport.
>
> b  Do you remember our trip to Colombia in 2010?
>
> c  I have a photo of you on the beach.

---

Reply  Forward  ✉

Hi Rafa,

**1** _____

We went to the beach in Santa Marta. We were there day and night because there were no hotels. It was great. It wasn't very expensive, and it was really beautiful. I'm writing to you because I have some pictures from the trip!

**2** _____

You're in the water 🌊 next to a really tall man, and you're wearing a new shirt. You were very cute. Do you remember the guy's name? I think he was from Canada. 🇨🇦

**3** _____

I'm wearing a long skirt with flowers. 🌸 The flowers on my skirt were red, yellow, and orange. Your shirt was pink and purple. I can't remember your shorts. They weren't very nice. Do you remember them? Do you have the photo? 📷

Love,

Ichiko

---

B  Read the sentences and check (✓) where emojis are correct.

1  (At the doctor's office) Can the doctor see me tomorrow? 😲  _____

2  (On social media) I was at work until 10:30 last night. 😠  _____

3  (In a text message) Do you want to get together on the weekend? 😲  _____

4  (At school) Professor Marumi, I'm not going to be in class next week. 😠

C  Write an email about a trip in the past. Use one paragraph for each idea. Write a topic sentence for each paragraph.

# CHECK AND REVIEW

**Read the statements. Can you do these things?**

| UNIT 11 | Mark the boxes. ☑ I can do it. ? I am not sure.<br>I can … | If you are not sure, go back to these pages in the Student's Book. |
|---|---|---|
| VOCABULARY | ☐ use adjectives to describe people, places, and things. | page 108 |
| | ☐ use words for colors. | page 110 |
| GRAMMAR | ☐ use statements with *was* and *were* | page 109 |
| | ☐ use questions with *was* and *were* | page 111 |
| FUNCTIONAL LANGUAGE | ☐ express uncertainty. | page 112 |
| | ☐ take time to think. | page 113 |
| SKILLS | ☐ use topic sentences in your writing. | page 115 |
| | ☐ write an email about an experience in the past. | page 115 |

# UNIT **12**   STOP, EAT, GO

## **12.1**   BACKPACKING AND SNACKING

**1** VOCABULARY: Snacks and small meals

A **Cross out the word that does <u>not</u> complete each sentence.**

1  I usually drink _____ juice with my breakfast.     apple     pineapple     ~~potato~~

2  _____ comes from an animal.     Chicken     Beef     Soup

3  _____ is a dairy product.     Lamb     Cheese     Butter

4  _____ is made from grain.     a cracker     a pineapple     bread

5  _____ are fruit that grow on trees.     Potatoes     Coconuts     Oranges

6  I often have _____ for lunch.     soup     sandwiches     butter

7  I use _____ to make vegetable soup.     tomatoes     potatoes     apples

**2** GRAMMAR: Simple past statements

A **Complete the sentences. Write the simple past form of the verbs.**

1  I like apples. I _____ liked _____ apples when I was a child.

2  They don't go to the supermarket on Saturday. They _____ to the supermarket last Saturday.

3  Elena tries a different restaurant every month. She _____ a different restaurant last month.

4  We eat bread every day. We _____ bread yesterday.

5  I don't drink tea at night. I _____ tea last night.

6  Max always buys food on Sunday. He _____ food last Sunday.

90

B  Change the affirmative (+) verbs so they're negative (–). Change the negative (–) verbs so they're affirmative (+).

1  I didn't eat beef. I _____ *ate* _____ chicken.

2  I didn't drink coffee. I _____ tea.

3  Ramon liked the Chinese restaurant. He _____ the French restaurant.

4  The bus didn't arrive at 10:15. It _____ at 10:20.

5  We went to the supermarket. We _____ to the park.

6  We didn't stop for lunch. We _____ for a snack.

## 3  GRAMMAR AND VOCABULARY

A  Write true affirmative (+) and negative (–) sentences about the past. Use the words in the box or your own ideas.

| | | | |
|---|---|---|---|
| apple/apples | butter | cracker/crackers | potato/potatoes |
| banana/bananas | cheese | lamb | sandwich/sandwiches |
| beef | chicken | orange/oranges | soup |
| bread | coconut/coconuts | pineapple/pineapples | tomato/tomatoes |

1  I / have / for dinner last night

   I had chicken for dinner last night. I didn't have lamb.

2  I / buy / last week

3  I / need / yesterday

4  I / like / when I was a child

5  I / want / last weekend

6  I / eat / for breakfast this morning

# WHAT DID YOU EAT?

## 1 VOCABULARY: Food, drinks, and desserts

A Find the words in the box in the word search.

| | |
|---|---|
| black beans | chocolate cake |
| cookies | eggs |
| fish | green beans |
| ice cream | juice |
| pizza | rice |
| soda | steak |
| water | |

| C | F | D | J | U | Z | G | R | Y | Z | K | W | P |
|---|---|---|---|---|---|---|---|---|---|---|---|---|
| O | F | J | A | G | P | R | H | S | O | D | A | L |
| O | C | O | B | J | R | E | G | Y | U | I | T | V |
| K | J | T | L | U | Q | E | Y | H | P | F | E | I |
| I | L | F | G | I | H | N | J | O | P | I | R | C |
| E | B | L | A | C | K | B | E | A | N | S | C | E |
| S | A | X | C | E | V | E | B | G | D | H | M | C |
| Z | D | P | P | I | Y | A | Y | R | G | J | S | R |
| W | A | A | I | J | K | N | O | Q | W | S | T | E |
| R | X | D | R | Z | K | S | H | S | A | F | E | A |
| I | H | B | S | T | Z | A | Z | C | V | R | A | M |
| C | H | O | C | O | L | A | T | E | C | A | K | E |
| E | F | U | O | P | T | F | J | E | M | G | K | M |

## 2 GRAMMAR: Simple past questions; *any*

A Complete the sentences with *some* or *any*.

1 I didn't have _____*any*_____ breakfast this morning.

2 Armando wanted _____ cookies last night.

3 Did you eat _____ rice yesterday?

4 We didn't have _____ homework last week.

5 I had _____ juice with my breakfast this morning.

6 Manolo went to the supermarket because he wanted to buy _____ fruit.

7 Were there _____ desserts at lunch?

8 My children didn't drink _____ soda with lunch.

B   Use the words to write questions about the past. Then answer the questions for you.

1   you / see / your friends / on the weekend
    Did you see your friends on the weekend?                    No, I didn't. They were working.

2   you and your family / have / dinner at home / last Friday


3   what / you / eat / yesterday


4   how / they / hear / about the new café


5   he / drink / soda / at breakfast


6   you / go / to the movie theatre / after dinner


7   where / she / buy / the pineapples


8   you / take / your friends / to your favorite restaurant / last month


## 3   GRAMMAR AND VOCABULARY

A   Write questions so the answers are true for you. Use the words in exercise 1A. You can use *any*.

1   A   Did you have any juice yesterday morning?
    B   Yes, I did. I had some orange juice.

2   A   _____ last week?
    B   No, I didn't. I don't like it, so I never drink it.

3   A   _____ yesterday afternoon?
    B   Yes, I did. I had some with lunch.

4   A   _____ yesterday?
    B   Yes, I did. I eat some every day.

5   A   Where _____?
    B   At the supermarket.

6   A   How _____?
    B   I didn't cook them. I never cook them.

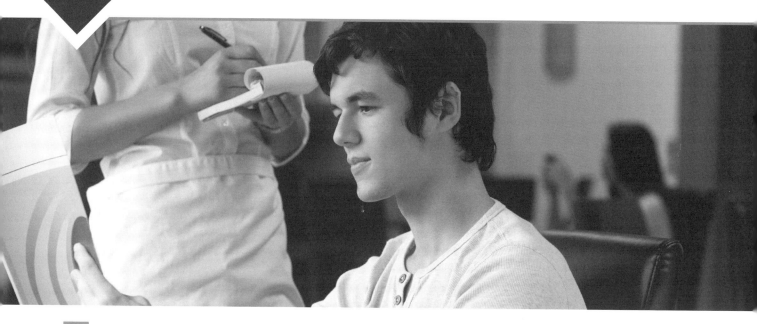

# 12.3 PLEASE PASS THE BUTTER

## 1 FUNCTIONAL LANGUAGE: Making and responding to offers and requests

A **Rewrite the sentences. Use *would like* or *'d like*.**

1  I want some fish, please.             *I would like (OR I'd like) some fish, please.*

2  Do you want some rice with the fish?

3  What do you want to drink?

4  When do you want the bread?

5  We want a table for six people.

6  Do you want a table near the window?

B **Circle the correct words.**

**Server**  Is everything OK?

**Endo**  ¹*I want water. / (Can I have some water, please?)*

**Server**  ²*Of course. / Thanks.* [ … ] ³*Here you are. / This is your food.*

**Endo**  Thank you. I ⁴*like / 'd like* some juice, too. ⁵*Do you have / How about* orange juice?

**Server**  I'm sorry. ⁶*We have / It's* orange soda but not orange juice. ⁷*Do / Would* you like some orange soda?

**Endo**  No, thanks. [ … ] Luis, please ⁸*take / pass* the bread.

**Luis**  ⁹*Here you are. / No, thank you.*

**Endo**  Thanks.

## 2 REAL-WORLD STRATEGY: Using *so* and *really* to make words stronger

A **Add *so* or *really* to the sentences.**

1  This chocolate cake is good.

2  I want to go to the pizza restaurant.

3  My cell phone is cool.

4  Our apartment is small.

5  I need a vacation!

94

## 3 FUNCTIONAL LANGUAGE AND REAL-WORLD STRATEGY

A  **Sandy is on a plane. Write the missing words in her conversation.**

**Jake**  Would you ¹_____like_____ something to drink?

**Sandy**  ²_____ you have juice?

**Jake**  We ³_____ apple juice and orange juice.

**Sandy**  ⁴_____ I have some apple juice, please?

**Jake**  ⁵_____ course. And what ⁶_____ you like for dinner? We
⁷_____ chicken or fish.

**Sandy**  I'd ⁸_____ the chicken, please.

**Jake**  Do you ⁹_____ green beans or black beans with the chicken?

**Sandy**  ¹⁰_____ like black beans, please.

**Jake**  ¹¹_____ you are.

**Sandy**  Thank you.

B  **Imagine you are on a plane. You are going to eat and drink something. Write a conversation with the
server. Say what you would like.**

_____

_____

_____

_____

_____

_____

_____

_____

## 1   LISTENING

A   🔊 **12.01**  **LISTEN FOR DETAILS**  Listen to Mia and Seb talking about hotels. Which hotel do they choose – Astoria Hotel, Capital Hotel, or White Doors Hotel?

_____

B   🔊 **12.01**  **LISTEN FOR SUPPORTING DETAILS**  Listen again. Match the hotels (1–3) with the correct information (a–f). You can use some information two times.

1   Astoria Hotel        _____
2   Capital Hotel        _____
3   White Doors Hotel    _____

a   It's expensive.
b   It's near the ocean.
c   It's on a quiet street.
d   People need a car for this hotel.
e   The reviews of the hotel restaurant are good.
f   The hotel always has great reviews.

## 2   READING

A   Read the hotel review. Write (+) next to the things the reviewer liked. Write (–) next to the things the reviewer didn't like. Write (✗) next to the things the reviewer did not write about.

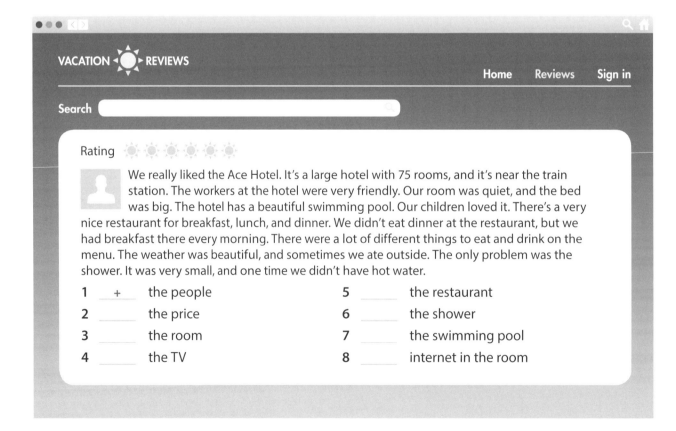

VACATION ☀ REVIEWS                                    Home      Reviews      Sign in

Search [                                        ]

Rating ☀ ☀ ☀ ☀ ☀ ☀

We really liked the Ace Hotel. It's a large hotel with 75 rooms, and it's near the train station. The workers at the hotel were very friendly. Our room was quiet, and the bed was big. The hotel has a beautiful swimming pool. Our children loved it. There's a very nice restaurant for breakfast, lunch, and dinner. We didn't eat dinner at the restaurant, but we had breakfast there every morning. There were a lot of different things to eat and drink on the menu. The weather was beautiful, and sometimes we ate outside. The only problem was the shower. It was very small, and one time we didn't have hot water.

1   _+_   the people
2   ____   the price
3   ____   the room
4   ____   the TV
5   ____   the restaurant
6   ____   the shower
7   ____   the swimming pool
8   ____   internet in the room

## 3 WRITING

A **Add commas to the sentences when necessary.**

1 We stayed at the hotel on Monday, Tuesday, and Wednesday.

2 The room was noisy and small.

3 We had lunch and dinner at the hotel.

4 The hotel is near popular restaurants cafés and stores.

5 The busy months at my job are May June and July.

6 I went with my brother my sister and my cousin.

B **Read the questions and answers. Check (✓) when the speaker answers his or her own question.**

| | | |
|---|---|---|
| 1 | Where did you stay? | At a hotel near the beach. |
| 2 | Am I happy? | Of course, I'm happy. |
| 3 | Did I like the chocolate cake? | I loved the chocolate cake! |
| 4 | Do you want some pizza? | No, thank you. I'd like a sandwich. |

C **Imagine you stayed at a hotel in your town. Write a review of the hotel. Describe the hotel and where it is. Say what is good (or bad) about the hotel.**

# CHECK AND REVIEW

**Read the statements. Can you do these things?**

| UNIT 12 | Mark the boxes. ☑ I can do it. ? I am not sure. I can … | If you are not sure, go back to these pages in the Student's Book. |
|---|---|---|
| VOCABULARY | ☐ use words for snacks and small meals. | page 118 |
| | ☐ use words for food, drinks, and desserts. | page 120 |
| GRAMMAR | ☐ use the simple past in statements. | page 119 |
| | ☐ use the simple past in *yes/no* and information questions. | page 121 |
| | ☐ use *any*. | page 121 |
| FUNCTIONAL LANGUAGE | ☐ offer and request food and drink. | page 122 |
| | ☐ use *so* and *really* to make words stronger. | page 123 |
| SKILLS | ☐ use commas in lists. | page 125 |
| | ☐ write a hotel review. | page 125 |

# EXTRA ACTIVITIES

**1** TIME TO SPEAK  People from history

A **Go online. Find information about the people in the photos in Student's Book lesson 1.5 (page 10).**
  - Find the people's jobs.
  - Find one other piece of information.
  - Write one sentence for each person. Say the job and one other thing.

**2** TIME TO SPEAK  What's true for me

A **Write sentences that are true for you and your friends.**
  - Write how you and your friends are the same.
  - Write how you are different.

B **Read your sentences to your class.**

**3** TIME TO SPEAK  A new home

A **Go online. Find something to buy for your home.**

B **Write three sentences about it. For example:**
  - It's an interesting color.
  - It's cool.
  - It's good for my desk.

C **Read your sentences to your class.**

**4** TIME TO SPEAK  Playlists

A **Go online. Find a song in English. Are the verbs from Unit 4 in the Student's Book in the song?**

B **Circle *a* or *an* in the words of the song.**

**5** TIME TO SPEAK  Life = 5 + 2

A **Go online and research the work week in three countries.**

B **How many days do people work? How many hours do they work?**

C **Read your sentences to your class.**

**6** TIME TO SPEAK  A good place to live

A **Look online for pictures of a city in your country or another country.**

B **Plan your visit. What places do you want to see in the city? What do you want to do in the city?**

C **Write about the things you want to do in the city.**

**7** TIME TO SPEAK  Your life these days

A  **Look online for books, movies, and songs.**

- What books are people reading these days?
- What movies are people watching these days?
- What songs are people listening to these days?

B  **Write sentences and read to your class.**

**8** TIME TO SPEAK  National skills

A  **People in these countries speak English. Choose <u>five</u> countries.**

- Australia
- Canada
- Ireland
- Jamaica
- New Zealand
- South Africa
- the United Kingdom
- the United States

B  **Write sentences about what people in each country can do really well.**

C  **Read your sentences to your class. Do other students agree?**

**9** TIME TO SPEAK  Vacation plans

A  **Make travel plans.**

- Where do you want to go?
- What do you want to do?
- What do you need to do to travel there?

*I want to go to San Diego … I want to swim and go to the zoo. I need to fly from my city.*

B  **Tell the class about your vacation plans.**

C  **Do other students have different ideas?**

**10** TIME TO SPEAK  48 hours in your city

A  **Imagine a group of college students is going to visit your city next month. Plan 48 hours in your city for the group. Make a list of interesting things they can do in your city.**

B  **Read your list to the class. Do you have the same ideas?**

**11** TIME TO SPEAK  TV memories

A  **Talk to your family and friends about their favorite childhood TV shows.**

B  **Go online and find information (names, places, things) about the shows.**

C  **Write sentences about the shows.**

D  **Read your sentences to your class. Did other students write sentences about the same shows?**

**12** TIME TO SPEAK  Recipe for a great restaurant

A  **Look online for a restaurant you want to visit.**

B  **Read reviews for the restaurant. What do people like about the restaurant? What do people <u>not</u> like?**

C  **Show the restaurant website to the class. Tell the class about the reviewers' comments.**

The authors and publishers acknowledge the following sources of copyright material and are grateful for the permissions granted. While every effort has been made, it has not always been possible to identify the sources of all the material used, or to trace all copyright holders. If any omissions are brought to our notice, we will be happy to include the appropriate acknowledgments on reprinting and in the next update to the digital edition, as applicable.

**Photo**
Key: B = Below, BL = Below Left, BR = Below Right, CL = Centre Left, CR = Centre Right, T = Top, TL = Top Left, TR = Top Right.

All photos are sourced from Getty Images.

p. 2: David Arky; p. 3, p. 8 (CL), p. 33, p. 50, p. 58 (Photo 4), p. 58 (Photo 12), p. 74, p. 27 (BR): Westend61; p. 4, p. 22: Caiaimage/Sam Edwards; p. 5, p. 14: Caiaimage/Tom Merton; p. 6: John Borthwick/Lonely Planet Images; p. 7: Eric Audras/ONOKY; p. 8 (TL): Tetra Images/Brand X Pictures; p. 8 (TR): Jose Luis Pelaez/Iconica; p. 8 (CR): Kali9/iStock/ Getty Images Plus; p. 11 (TR): Juanmonino/E+; p. 11 (B): Tom Merton/ Caiaimage; p. 12 (old): Sally Anscombe/Moment; p. 12 (boaring): LWA/ Dann Tardif/Blend Images; p. 12 (short): Paperboat/E+; p. 12 (shy): Imagenavi; p. 12 (funny): Hollie Fernando/DigitalVision; p. 12 (reading): Tim Hall/The Image Bank; p. 12 (friendly): Robert Daly/OJO Images; p. 12 (couple): Ken Chernus/Photodisc; p. 12 (kid): Emma Kim/Cultura; p. 12 (boy): William King/Taxi; p. 12 (woman): Blend Images - Hill Street Studios/Brand X Pictures; p. 15 (TR): Tim Macpherson/Cultura; p. 15 (B): PhotoAlto/Sigrid Olsson/PhotoAlto Agency RF Collections; p. 16: Sjenner13/iStock/Getty Images Plus; p. 20 (photo 1): Johner Images; p. 20 (photo 2): ExperienceInteriors/iStock/Getty Images Plus; p. 20 (photo 3): Spaces Images/Blend Images; p. 20 (photo 4): Andreas von Einsiedel/ Corbis Documentary; p. 21: AJ_Watt/E+; p. 23: Alena Gamm/EyeEm; p. 24 (Photo 1): Jeremy Walker/Photographer's Choice; p. 24 (Photo 2): Luiz Souza/NurPhoto/Getty Images; p. 26 (photo 1): Pagadesign/E+; p. 26 (photo 2): Alexander Spatari/Moment; p. 26 (photo 3): Hudiemm/ E+; p. 26 (photo 4): alexsl/iStock/Getty Images; p. 26 (photo 5): Mrgao/ iStock/Getty Images; p. 26 (photo 6): Howard Kingsnorth/The Image Bank; p. 26 (photo 7): Davidscar/iStock/Getty Images Plus; p. 26 (photo 8): Dave King/Dorling Kindersley; p. 27 (T): Oneclearvision/iStocK/ Getty Images Plus; p. 28: Squaredpixels/E+; p. 29 (TR), p. 43, p. 51, p. 85 (girl): Hero Images; p. 29 (B): JGI/Tom Grill/Blend Images; p. 30: Tetra Images; p. 31: Deborah Kolb/Blend Images; p. 32 (CR): Topic Images Inc; p. 32 (B): Chris Ryan/Caiaimage; p. 35: Kali9/iStock/E+; p. 37: Shannon Fagan/Blend Images; p. 38: NicolasMcComber/E+; p. 40: Heide Benser/Corbis; p. 41: Sangfoto/iStock/Getty Images Plus; p. 42: Maremagnum/Photolibrary; p. 44 (TL): Rachid Dahnoun; p. 44 (CL): Joe daniel price/Moment; p. 44 (TR): Svjetlana/RooM; p. 44 (CR): Laszlo Podor/Moment; p. 45: Jhorrocks/iStock/Getty Images Plus; p. 46: Krakozawr/iStocK/Getty Images Plus; p. 48: Ferrantraite/Vetta; p. 49: David Bank/AWL Images; p. 52: M_a_y_a/E+; p. 54: DMEPhotography/ iStock/Getty Images Plus; p. 55: Fresh Meat Media LLC/The Image Bank; p. 56: Jim Craigmyle/Corbis; p. 58 (photo 1): Efenzi/E+; p. 58 (photo 2): Ruth Jenkinson/Dorling Kindersley; p. 58 (photo 3): Flyfloor/E+; p. 58 (Photo 5): MCCAIG/iStock/Getty Images Plus; p. 58 (Photo 6): otnaydur/Shutterstock; p. 58 (Photo 7): Kevin Smith/Perspectives; p. 58 (Photo 8): Jerry Driendl/The Image Bank; p. 58 (Photo 9): JGI/Blend Images; p. 58 (Photo 10): Caiaimage/Sam Edwards/OJO+; p. 58 (Photo 11): Jose Luis Pelaez Inc/Blend Images; p.58 (waves): Specker/Vedfelt/ Taxi; p. 60: Skynesher/E+; p. 61: Monkeybusinessimages/iStock/Getty Images Plus; p. 62: PeopleImages/E+; p. 63: Steve Debenport/iStock/ Getty Images Plus; p. 66: Tim Boyle/Getty Images; p. 67 (TR): Saro17/ E+; p. 67 (CL): RachelDewis/iStock/Getty Images Plus; p. 67 (BR): Jose Fuste Raga/Corbis Documentary; p. 68: Studio 504/Stone; p. 69: Marco Brivio/Photographer's Choice RF; p. 70: Hiya Images/Corbis/VCG/ Corbis; p. 71, p. 92: Andresr/E+; p. 72: GUY Christian/Hemis.fr; p. 75: Troy Aossey/Taxi; p. 76: Seanscott/RooM; p. 77: 97/E+; p. 78: Seb Oliver/ Image Source; p. 80 (T): Bjorn Andren; p. 80 (BL): NightAndDayImages/ E+; p. 80 (BR): Ken Ross/VW Pics/UIG/Getty Images; p. 83: JTB Photo/ UIG/Getty Images; p. 84: Daniele Carotenuto Photography/Moment; p. 85 (shoe): Peter Dazeley/Photographer's Choice; p. 86: Thomas Barwick/ Taxi; p. 88: Switch/ailead/amana images; p. 90: GUIZIOU Franck/ hemispicture.com/hemis.fr; p. 91: David Nevala/Aurora; p. 93 (T): Eileen Bach/Iconica; p. 93 (BR): Rosemary Calvert/Photographer's Choice RF; p. 94: Wavebreakmedia/iStock/Getty Images Plus; p. 95: Zoranm/E+; p. 96: LOOK Photography/UpperCut Images; p. 19: Nikada/E+; p. 64: Kohei Hara/DigitalVision; p. 82: Erik Isakson/Blend Images; p. 87: Luis Alvarez/Taxi.

Below image is sourced from Shutterstock.
p. 58 (Photo 6): otnaydur/Shutterstock.

Front cover photography by Arctic-Images/The Image Bank/Getty Images.

**Illustration**
Alejandro Mila (Sylvie Poggio Artists Agency) pp. 18, 47.

**Audio**
Audio production by CityVox, New York.

**Corpus**
Development of this publication has made use of the Cambridge English Corpus (CEC). The CEC is a multi-billion word collection of contemporary spoken and written English. It includes British English, American English, and other varieties. It also includes the Cambridge Learner Corpus, the world's biggest collection of learner writing, developed in collaboration with Cambridge Assessment. Cambridge University Press uses the CEC to provide evidence about language use that helps to produce better language teaching materials. Our Evolve authors study the Corpus to see how English is really used, and to identify typical learner mistakes. This information informs the authors' selection of vocabulary, grammar items and Student's Book Corpus features such as the Accuracy Check, Register Check, and Insider English.